# Options Trading

# Interview Questions

# Options Trading Interview Questions

Hugh Calloway

BridgeView Recruiting

*To those studying for trading interviews...*

*Remember that nobody actually computes Black Scholes by hand, but everyone pretends they could. The real test is whether you stay calm while doing trivial arithmetic under mild psychological pressure.*

# Preface

**Preface**

If you interviewed for an options trading job in the early 1990s, the first question was not about $E[x]$, or variance swaps, or jump diffusion. The first question was whether you could survive on the floor.

You learned to read lips and body language across a noisy pit. You memorized hand signals. You ran theoretical values off a pocket calculator and a laminated cheat sheet. You learned that the guy who looked calm when volatility exploded was either very good or completely blown out and hiding it. Either way, you watched him closely.

Most of the edge came from being faster with your mouth and your hands than the person next to you. Models mattered, but they were simple enough to live in your head. Time on the job taught you the rest. If you could quote, hedge, and not panic, you had a career.

Today, if you show up to an options trading interview with only that kind of edge, you will not make it past the first round.

Modern options markets are electronic, fragmented, and brutally efficient. Quotes stream at microsecond intervals. Automated market makers recycle their risk profile thousands of times a day. A large part of total volume is driven by algorithms negotiating basis points and microstructure noise. Even in listed equity options, the landscape looks more like a low latency engineering problem than a shouting match.

Yet the questions have not become simpler. They have become different.

Instead of asking whether you know how to price a call, interviewers ask what happens to your gamma profile if the exchange halts underlying trading in the middle of an event. Instead of asking you to define delta, they will ask you how your hedging strategy changes as realized volatility collapses even while implied volatility stays bid. Instead of asking for Black Scholes, they will ask why it fails, where it fails, and what you do about it when the model is wrong and the market is right.

This book exists for that environment.

It is not a textbook, and it is not a collection of clever riddles for their own sake. It is a map of the conversations you are likely to have when you sit down across from someone who has risk on and wants to know whether you can help manage it.

Over the past thirty years, three forces have reshaped the role of the options trader.

The first is technology. The old floor based edge of seeing order flow before the rest of the world has largely been replaced by co located servers and smart order routers. Execution quality now comes from your ability to design and calibrate systems rather than shout the right size at the right moment. A modern interview reflects that. You may be asked to derive an options Greek, and then in the next breath explain how you would approximate that same sensitivity quickly enough to feed it into an intraday risk engine. You may see questions about simulation, Monte Carlo, or backtesting, not as academic exercises, but as tools you will use every day.

The second is regulation. Over time, capital and margin rules, electronic audit trails, and post crisis reforms have changed the cost of carrying risk and the shape of liquidity. A trader today has to understand not just how to construct a position, but how that position is treated by clearing, by risk, and by the regulator. An interview can easily wander into questions about stress scenarios, concentration limits, and how to design trades that are efficient not only in *P&L* space but in capital space. You are not expected to be a lawyer. You are expected to understand the environment where your trades live.

The third is the profile of market participants. The growth of online brokers and inexpensive trading tools has pulled a large mass of retail flow into the options markets. Some of it is hedging. Some of it is speculation. All of it shapes order flow and implied volatility. At the same time, institutional strategies have become more systematic. Volatility targeting, risk premia harvesting, and structured product issuance have turned what used to be occasional flows into steady, programmatic patterns.

You see the impact of this most clearly in the recent explosion of zero days to expiration trading. Same day expiry options used to be an end of day curiosity. Now in some indices they can make up the majority of daily volume. That reality shows up in interviews. You might be asked how intraday gamma scalping works when your entire book expires at the close. You might be asked how to think about tail risk and gap risk when your holding period is measured in hours. You might be asked how to separate signal from noise when most of the tape is very short dated optionality turning over again and again.

Underneath all of that, the core of the job has not changed as much as it appears.

You still need to understand how options behave. You still need to know why a call is convex, why short vega feels comfortable until it does not, why a skew is steep and what could flatten it. You still need a feel for how a book will react when the underlying moves three standard deviations and liquidity vanishes. You still need to balance the neat closed forms of pricing theory with the messy reality that markets do whatever they like.

The difference is that the bar has been raised. The modern trader is expected to be fluent in both worlds. The intuition that used to be enough must now be paired with quantitative literacy. Interviewers look for candidates who can move comfortably between a whiteboard derivation, a back of the envelope estimate, and a practical discussion of how to execute a trade efficiently with the tools at hand.

That is why this book is framed around questions.

An interview is a compressed conversation. In a short span of time, your counterpart wants to see how you think about risk, uncertainty, and incomplete information. Well designed questions give them a window into your process. Well prepared answers give you a way to demonstrate that you have done the work.

You will see questions that start gently and then dig deeper. A simple query about put call parity can lead naturally into discussions about funding rates, short sale constraints, or dislocations during market stress. A warm up on $E[x]$ and variance can turn into a conversation about realized versus implied volatility, or about how to construct and hedge a straddle in a market where borrowing stock is difficult. A straightforward setup on the Greeks often becomes a probe into how you would hedge across multiple underlyings, maturities, and strike clusters when the usual assumptions break down.

If you are new to options, you can use these questions to build a foundation. If you are already trading, you can use them to sharpen your narrative and fill in gaps. In both cases, the goal is the same. By the time you walk into the interview, none of the core topics should be entirely unfamiliar, and you should have already wrestled with the kinds of follow ups that good interviewers tend to ask.

You will not find every exotic corner of the industry represented here. There are as many flavors of options trading roles as there are desks. Market making in index options, relative value in single names, volatility arbitrage, structured products, corporate derivatives, and buy side overlay management each carry their own jargon and customs. What you will find are the common threads. The mechanics of pricing and hedging. The logic of risk management. The intuition behind why markets sometimes behave in ways that seem irrational and yet recur again and again.

Over the years, I have watched bright candidates stumble on simple questions because they had memorized formulas without understanding them. I have also watched others recover from early mistakes by thinking clearly in real time. Interviewers are often less interested in whether you know the exact coefficient in a density function than in whether you can reason from first principles when something does not look right.

Treat the questions in this book as prompts to practice that reasoning. Do not just read the solutions. Pause and write out your own. Challenge yourself to extend each idea. Ask how it changes if transaction costs rise, if liquidity dries up, if the underlying starts paying a dividend, or if the exchange suddenly lists daily expiries in a product that used to have only monthlies. The market will certainly throw such variations at you. The interview is only a rehearsal.

The role of the options trader has moved from the noise of the pit to the hum of the server rack. The job is still, at its core, about making decisions under uncertainty with real money on the line. If this book does its job, you will walk into the interview with a clearer sense of what that responsibility entails and how to talk about it.

The rest will be up to you.

# Chapter 1: Payoffs, Intuition, and How Interviewers Actually Think

Walk into a derivatives interview, and you're not really being tested on whether you can recite Black–Scholes. You're being tested on whether you can look at a payoff and immediately feel what it wants to do. This chapter is about that feeling—how to think the way an options trader thinks when they see a call, a put, a forward, or a simple spread drawn on a whiteboard and they have to speak intelligently before the marker ink is dry.

On the surface, options theory looks like mathematics. Underneath, on an actual trading floor, it is language. Payoff diagrams are that language's alphabet. A vanilla call is the simplest way of saying "I like upside, but I respect my downside." A put says "I fear a crash more than I fear missing a rally." A forward whispers "no convexity here, just a straight bet on direction." A spread, with its rising and flattening lines, says "I want to participate, but only up to a point; beyond that, I don't care." Interviewers are listening for whether you can "read" these sentences and respond in kind, even when the numbers are fuzzy or the question is verbal rather than drawn.

The curious part is that most interviews start with problems that barely require arithmetic. "Stock is 100. You buy a 105 call. Stock goes to 200. Who's happier: you or the person who sold it to you?" Or: "You're long a forward and own the stock. What risks are you actually taking?" These are not trick questions; they are X-rays. They show whether you understand direction (which way you want the underlying to move), leverage (how much that move matters to your P&L), and convexity (how your happiness accelerates or decelerates as the underlying drifts away from the strike). If you instinctively talk about linear versus nonlinear exposure, or how small moves matter less than big ones in an option, you are already much closer to the trading desk's mindset than someone who can derive a pricing formula but can't explain why a call option holder sleeps better than a levered stock investor.

On real desks, traders reduce complex books to simple mental pictures. A portfolio of exotics might be summarized as "long downside convexity, short upside skew," which in plain English might be: "We get hurt slowly if the market grinds higher, but we bleed quickly if volatility disappears." They get there by decomposing everything into forwards, calls, puts, and spreads. That is why interviewers obsess over basic payoff intuition; it's the foundation on which all those mental summaries rest. If you can linearly combine a few simple payoffs in your head, you can mentally rebuild most of the structures they actually trade.

There is another unspoken reason interviewers care about payoff intuition: it reveals how you think under uncertainty. Consider a question like, "You sell an at-the-money straddle. If the stock doesn't move for a week, are you guaranteed to make money?" Do you rush to answer "yes" because time decay sounds good for a seller? Or do you pause, recognize that unchanged spot does not mean unchanged option price, and bring in volatility, skew, and interest rates as possible culprits? Even if you don't fully quantify those effects, showing that you know the payoff picture is only the beginning, not the end, of the story, signals that you can grow into a risk-taker's role.

It's tempting to think that being clever means jumping straight to Greeks and formulas. In reality, many of the hardest questions in interviews—and on the desk—can be framed and half-solved with a crude, childlike drawing: a kink at the strike for a call, a straight line for a forward, a tent shape for a butterfly, a plateau for a capped spread. From these pictures alone, you can say who wins when the market rallies, who bleeds when it chops sideways, where leverage explodes, and where risk quietly dies out. That's exactly the level at which your interviewer is operating when they fire off a "what happens if...?" scenario.

As you go through this chapter, expect questions that sound almost disappointingly simple. "Is this structure long or short volatility?" "Would you prefer a call or a forward if you're bullish but nervous?" "How does combining a long call and a short put at the same strike feel compared to a forward?" Beneath their simplicity lies the real filter: can you reason your way through direction, convexity, and leverage, without hiding behind a formula? Once you can, every later topic—delta-hedging, volatility trading, exotic payoff engineering—stops being mysterious math and becomes an extension of this core intuition.

## 1.1: Interview Questions

### 1.1.1: Question 1.1

**Question:** If you predict that the volatility of a stock will be 10% a year from now, and the current price is $X$ dollars, how would you hedge this risk?

**Intuition:**

You are making a view not on the direction of the stock, but on how much it will move (its volatility). "Hedging this risk" really means: structure a position whose profit depends on whether realized volatility over the next year ends up above or below the market's implied volatility today, while staying (roughly) insensitive to the stock's price level. You do that with options and by neutralizing their directional exposure.

**Solution:**

Let current stock price be $S_0 = X$ and your forecast of future annualized volatility be $\sigma^* = 10\%$. The market prices options using an implied volatility $\sigma_{\text{mkt}}$ extracted from option prices via a model such as Black–Scholes.

If you believe $\sigma^* < \sigma_{\text{mkt}}$, you think options are "too expensive" on a volatility basis. You would sell volatility: for example, sell at-the-money options (calls, puts, or straddles) whose prices $C(S_0, K, T, \sigma_{\text{mkt}})$ or $P(S_0, K, T, \sigma_{\text{mkt}})$ embed implied volatility above 10%.

Since these options have delta $\Delta \neq 0$, you make the position delta-neutral by trading the stock. For a short option position with total delta $\Delta_{\text{opt}}$, you buy or sell stock so that total delta is near zero:

$$\Delta_{\text{total}} = \Delta_{\text{opt}} + \Delta_{\text{stock}} \approx 0.$$

You then rebalance this hedge over time (delta-hedging). Your P&L over the hedge horizon decomposes into terms driven by realized volatility versus implied volatility. Profit arises if realized volatility $\sigma_{\text{real}}$ is close to your forecast 10%, and in particular if

$$\sigma_{\text{real}} < \sigma_{\text{mkt}},$$

because you sold options at "too high" implied volatility and then hedged away most directional risk.

Conversely, if you believe $\sigma^* > \sigma_{\text{mkt}}$, you buy options (e.g., a long straddle), then delta-hedge. You gain if realized volatility ends up exceeding the market's implied volatility.

**Logic:**
The algorithm is: first infer the market's implied volatility from option prices; compare it to your forecast 10%; decide whether to be long or short options; construct a delta-neutral portfolio by offsetting option delta with stock; and keep rebalancing the hedge so the P&L becomes primarily a function of realized versus implied volatility, not of the stock's direction.

**Common Mistake:**
Candidates often talk about simply buying or selling options based on a volatility view but ignore delta-hedging. Without delta-hedging, the position's P&L is dominated by directional moves in $S$, not by whether realized volatility matches the forecast. Another frequent miss is to ignore the difference between your forecast and implied volatility;

your forecast alone is meaningless unless you compare it to what is already priced in.

## 1.1.2: Question 1.2

**Question:** In dynamic hedging, how is profit captured, and what is the source of this profit?

**Answer:** Profit in dynamic hedging is captured through repeated rebalancing of a delta-hedged option position as the underlying price $S$ moves. You hold an option with gamma and hedge its delta by trading the underlying so that total delta stays near zero. When realized volatility of $S$ differs from the volatility implied in the option price, the cumulative gains from these hedge adjustments plus the option payoff differ from the initial option cost. If you are long gamma and realized volatility exceeds implied, the frequent buy-low/sell-high rebalancing in $S$ generates trading profits. Thus, the source of profit is the discrepancy between implied and realized volatility, monetized via gamma and dynamic re-hedging.

## 1.1.3: Question 1.3

**Question:** How can Asian options be hedged using European call options?

**Intuition:** An Asian option's payoff depends on the average of the underlying price over time, while a European call depends only on the terminal price at maturity. To hedge an Asian option with Europeans, you try to approximate the exposure to this average by trading European calls at different strikes and times to maturity so that the portfolio's sensitivity to the underlying path resembles that of the Asian. In practice this is done dynamically: as the running average evolves, you rebalance a portfolio of European options and possibly the underlying to keep its risk profile close to that of the Asian option.

**Solution:** Consider a fixed-strike Asian call with maturity $T$ on an underlying price process $S_t$ and averaging dates $t_1, \dots, t_n$. Its payoff is

$$\text{Payoff}_A = \left( \frac{1}{n} \sum_{i=1}^{n} S_{t_i} - K \right)^+.$$

A European call with maturity $T$ and strike $K$ has payoff

$$\text{Payoff}_E = (S_T - K)^+.$$

The key observation is that $\frac{1}{n}\sum_{i=1}^{n} S_{t_i}$ is a linear functional of the path, while European option prices can be written as expectations of terminal payoffs under the risk-neutral measure. In a complete model like Black–Scholes, any square-integrable payoff can be replicated by a dynamic trading strategy in the underlying and a continuum of European options. Formally, one writes the Asian payoff as

$$\left( \frac{1}{n} \sum_{i=1}^{n} S_{t_i} - K \right)^+$$

$$= \int_0^{\infty} (S_T - k)^+ \, \phi(k) \, dk$$

$$+ \text{ dynamic stock/bond terms},$$

for some weight function $\phi(k)$ obtained via standard static replication arguments (Breeden–Litzenberger type results). In practice, you approximate this integral with a finite sum:

$$\text{Asian} \approx \sum_j w_j \, C(T, K_j),$$

where $C(T, K_j)$ is a European call with strike $K_j$, and $w_j$ are chosen so that the portfolio's Greeks (especially delta and gamma over time) match those of the Asian as closely as possible. You then rebalance this portfolio through time as the averaging window progresses.

**Logic:** Start from the path-dependent payoff. Express it as a function of the distribution of $S_T$ using risk-neutral pricing. Use the fact that any payoff can be decomposed into a static portfolio of European calls across strikes plus dynamic trading in the underlying. Approximate the static part with a discrete set of European calls, then dynamically adjust positions to maintain hedge quality as the running average changes.

**Common Mistake:** Candidates often say "you can't hedge Asians with Europeans because they're path-dependent." They ignore that in continuous-time complete markets, path-dependent payoffs can be replicated using dynamic strategies and a strip of Europeans; the challenge is practical approximation, not theoretical impossibility.

## 1.1.4: Question 1.4

**Question:** Under what circumstances would you consider early exercising an American call option?

**Answer:** Early exercise of an American call is almost never optimal on a non-dividend-paying stock because you lose remaining time value. It becomes worth considering mainly when the underlying pays dividends. If a sizable dividend will be paid before expiration, and the option is deep in-the-money so that its time value is very small, exercising just before the ex-dividend date can be optimal: you gain the dividend as a stockholder, which can outweigh the lost time value and the cost of paying the strike early. Practically, early exercise is considered when the call is deep in-the-money, close to ex-dividend, with low remaining time value and low interest-rate benefit from deferring the strike payment.

## 1.1.5: Question 1.5

**Question:** Why is delta-hedging a far-out-of-the-money options position considered dangerous? Which position is more dangerous, long or short?

**Answer:** Delta-hedging far-out-of-the-money options is dangerous because the option's delta is very small and changes rapidly when the underlying starts to move. You are effectively "flat" until a big move happens, then gamma kicks in and delta shifts sharply, forcing you to rebalance at the worst times and potentially in large size. This makes the hedge unreliable and transaction-cost intensive, and you are heavily exposed to gap risk and volatility shocks. Between long and short, the short far-OTM option is more dangerous: limited premium collected but potentially very large or unlimited losses if the underlying makes a big move into the strike region.

## 1.1.6: Question 1.6

**Question:** Can a call option have a delta greater than 100%?

**Answer:** Under the standard Black–Scholes framework for a vanilla call on a non-dividend-paying stock, delta lies between 0 and 1 (0%–100%), so it cannot exceed 100%. Delta is $\Delta = \frac{\partial C}{\partial S}$, where $C$ is the call price and $S$ is the underlying price.

However, *effective* or *position* delta can exceed 1 when you consider leveraged or structured products (e.g., options on futures, deep in-the-money options embedded in products, or portfolios of options). In those cases, the total sensitivity of your position to $S$ can be greater than 1, but the single vanilla call option's theoretical delta itself does not exceed 1.

## 1.1.7: Question 1.7

**Question:** How can options traders capture volatility mispricing using straddles?

**Answer:** Traders use at-the-money straddles (long call + long put with same strike and expiry) to bet that future realized volatility will exceed implied volatility. If the market's implied volatility $IV$ is too low relative to the trader's forecast of realized volatility $RV$, they buy the straddle. The profit driver is that option prices scale with volatility: roughly, higher $RV$ than $IV$ makes the straddle's gamma and vega pay off through large price swings. After volatility is realized or *IV* rises, they unwind (sell) the straddle at a higher price. Net profit is straddle payoff minus initial premium and transaction costs; success requires *RV* > *IV* by more than these costs.

# Chapter 2: Plain Vanilla Options, Put–Call Parity, and Arbitrage Bounds

Few financial instruments are as deceptively simple—and as endlessly revealing—as plain vanilla European options. On the surface, they are just standardized bets on the future value of a single underlying asset at a single maturity date. Yet from this modest setup emerges an intricate logic that governs what can and cannot be true in any rational market. This chapter is about learning to think inside that logic, quickly and under pressure.

You will see that once you fix the underlying, the maturity, and the strike, call and put prices are no longer free to wander independently. They are tied together by a surprisingly tight algebraic relationship: put–call parity. Traders use it almost subconsciously. Hand them two quotes—a call price and an interest rate, say—and they can tell you, within seconds, what the corresponding put "should" be worth if there is no arbitrage. What looks like a neat pricing identity is, in fact, a consistency condition on the entire market: if parity is violated, someone can build a portfolio that starts with cash in hand and no risk thereafter.

Behind that elegance lies the broader machinery of no-arbitrage bounds. Even without specifying a model for the underlying's dynamics—no Black–Scholes, no stochastic calculus—you can say a lot about where option prices must lie. A call cannot be worth less than its intrinsic value, otherwise you could buy the option and lock in a profit by immediately exercising in states where it is obviously beneficial. It cannot be worth more than the underlying itself, otherwise you could short the asset and buy the option, guaranteeing that you will never need to pay back more than what you've received. From a few such basic constructions, entire regions of the price space become "forbidden," not by regulation or convention but by pure logic.

One of the more curious aspects of this subject is how much information you can extract from very sparse data. Suppose you are given only the price of a call, the current underlying price, and a risk-free rate. With parity, you can infer the consistent put price. With bounds, you can check whether either quote is even plausible. You can often back out an implied forward price of the asset or detect that an interest rate assumption must be wrong if the quotes are to make sense. In hectic markets, experienced traders routinely perform these mental inversions, spotting misalignments not by scanning pages of data but by noticing a single number that "doesn't fit" with the rest.

The history of modern derivatives trading is filled with stories of firms exploiting tiny, fleeting violations of these relationships. In the early days of exchange-traded options, put–call parity was occasionally off by enough to allow for clean, nearly riskless arbitrage: long the cheap side, short the expensive side, hedge with the underlying, and wait for convergence. Nowadays, with algorithms enforcing consistency across venues in milliseconds, pure parity violations have become rare and short-lived. Yet the underlying reasoning remains the same, and when markets become stressed or illiquid—during crises, after major announcements—cracks can reappear, and those who can reason clearly under uncertainty find opportunities where others see only noise.

This chapter will train you to operate in that mindset. You will be dropped into scenarios where key pieces are missing, and your task will be to reconstruct them using only the tools of no-arbitrage reasoning. You will have to decide, from just a handful of numbers, whether a set of quotes is feasible or impossible, whether a mispricing is real or merely apparent once financing and dividends are accounted for, whether a trade that seems free of risk is actually hiding a subtle exposure. The aim is not just to memorize formulas, but to internalize the economic stories behind them: which portfolios are secretly the same, which cash flows can be replicated by others, and how prices must line up if those equivalences are to hold.

By the end, plain vanilla European options will feel less like simple one-off bets and more like pieces of a tightly interlocked system. You will see how a single misaligned quote can reveal an arbitrage, how modest assumptions about interest rates and dividends shape entire regions of admissible prices, and how parity and bounds act as a kind of grammar for the language of options. Once you are fluent in that grammar, you will not only recognize impossible prices—you will know exactly how to profit from them, or at least when to step aside because the market is telling you that something important remains unseen.

## 2.1: Interview Questions

### 2.1.1: Question 2.1

**Question:** You're interviewing for an index options market-making role. The index is at 100. You have a mild bullish view over the next month: you think the index is slightly more likely to end up between 102 and 108 than the market is pricing, but you don't have a strong view on big moves beyond 110. You also face a capital constraint: your desk head doesn't want you tying up too much balance sheet in outright delta.

You have liquid 1-month European calls and puts at strikes 95, 100, 105, and 110. You can also trade the underlying.

1) Propose a simple options structure (possibly combined with underlying) that best expresses your view while respecting the capital constraint. Be specific about long/short directions at which strikes.

2) Using replication intuition, decompose your structure into: (a) net delta position, and (b) a combination of vertical spreads (bull/bear spreads).

3) Based on that decomposition, explain in plain language what set of terminal payoffs you are actually long and short, and why this matches your qualitative view better than just buying the underlying.

**Answer:** A clean structure is: long $1 \times 100$ call, short $1.5 \times 105$ calls, long $0.5 \times 110$ calls. Equivalently, you are long $1 \times 100$–105 call spread and short $0.5 \times 105$–110 call spread. This gives modest positive delta near 100 and concentrates payoff between about 100 and 108, with capped exposure above 110.

In replication terms, net you own a capped bull spread from 100 to 105 and are half-short a further bull spread from 105 to 110, so your delta is positive but limited and falls off above 105–110.

Economically, you are long payoffs in the 100–105 region, partially long 105–110, and largely flat beyond 110, which matches "slightly bullish around spot, no strong view on large upside" better than simply buying the index, and uses less capital with limited downside (premium only).

## 2.1.2: Question 2.2

**Question:** You are shown a trade idea from a sales desk on a non-dividend-paying stock currently at 50. They propose the following 6-month structure (all European options, same maturity): - Long 1x 45 put - Long 1x 55 call - Short 2x 50 calls

They pitch it as: "You're roughly delta-neutral, with limited downside, and you make money if the stock ends up either below 45 or above 55."

1) Using replication logic and put–call parity (no formulas needed beyond the basic parity relation), decompose this payoff into simpler pieces involving the underlying and standard vertical spreads.

2) Based on that decomposition, is the sales pitch qualitatively accurate? In particular, does this structure really benefit from *both* big downside and big upside moves? Explain the main directional and convexity exposures in words, without calculating exact payoffs for every scenario.

Assume a zero interest rate environment for simplicity.

**Answer:** Using parity $C(45) - P(45) = S - 45$, the long 45 put is $P(45) = C(45) - S + 45$. Plugging in, the structure is: long $C(45)$, long $C(55)$, short $2C(50)$, and short $S$, plus a constant 45. The option part is a (slightly skewed) long call butterfly around 50: long 45–50 call spread plus long 50–55 call spread. Net: long convexity around 50, but short 1× underlying. So the trade is actually short-delta with long gamma near 50. It does not cleanly profit from both big downside and big upside: deep upside hurts (short stock plus flattened butterfly), and downside gains are limited, not an outright "long crash" profile. The sales pitch is therefore misleading.

## 2.1.3: Question 2.3

**Question:** You are trading options on a stock at 100. You believe the market underestimates the probability of a moderate downside move to around 90, but you don't think a crash to 70 is much more likely than the market does. In other words, you are bearish, but mainly on the 90–100 region, not on extreme tails.

You can trade 3-month European puts with strikes 90 and 100, and the underlying itself.

1) Propose an options structure that better matches your view than simply shorting the stock.

2) Using payoff and replication intuition (no formulas), explain how your structure can be seen as a combination of: (a) a stock position, and (b) a portfolio of digital-like payoffs concentrated in the 90–100 region.

3) Briefly explain why your structure is a more efficient expression of your view than either (i) shorting the stock or (ii) buying a deep out-of-the-money 70 put.

**Answer:** Use a 100–90 bear put spread: long the 100 put, short the 90 put. This pays off linearly as $S$ falls from 100 to 90, then flattens below 90, so you only "bet" on the 90–100 band and don't buy extra crash protection. Intuitively, the linear payoff between 90 and 100 is like being short stock only in that region; the flat 10 below 90 is like a digital that triggers once $S \leq 90$, with no further crash sensitivity. This structure is more efficient because it concentrates notional and premium where your edge is (90–100), unlike a stock short (which exposes you everywhere) or a 70 put (which mainly pays in a tail you don't claim to misprice).

## 2.1.4: Question 2.4

**Question:** A junior trader suggests the following 1-year structure on a non-dividend-paying stock at 100, all European options, same maturity: - Long 1x 90 put - Long 1x 110 call - Short 2x 100 straddles (i.e., short 2x 100 calls and short 2x 100 puts)

They claim: "This is a cheap way to be short volatility around 100 but long tail risk in both directions; I'll make money if the stock stays around 100, and I'm protected if it moves a lot."

1) Use replication thinking and put–call parity to rewrite this position as a combination of: (a) a position in the underlying, (b) a butterfly or combination of vertical spreads, and (c) any residual simple option structures.

2) Based on this decomposition, assess whether the stated risk description is directionally and convexity-wise correct. In particular:
    o   Are you genuinely long both upside and downside *tails*?
    o   Are you truly short volatility only "around 100," or more broadly?

3) Highlight one non-obvious risk in this structure that would likely surprise the junior trader after a large move in the underlying.

**Answer:** Start from +P(90) +C(110) −2C(100) −2P(100). Using $C(100) - P(100) = S - 100$ gives $-2C(100) -2P(100) = -4C(100) +2S -200$. So, up to cash: $P(90) + C(110) - 4C(100) + 2S$.

Using parity at 90: $P(90) = C(90) - S + 90$. Ignoring cash, this is $C(90) + C(110) - 4C(100) + S$.

Rewrite as $[\,C(90) + C(110) - 2C(100)\,] + [\,S - 2C(100)\,]$. The bracketed terms are: long 90–100–110 call butterfly, plus long 1× stock and short 2× 100 calls (a covered call with one extra short call).

You are not long both tails: downside is long stock vs one 90 put, upside has unbounded short-call risk beyond 100. You are short volatility broadly, especially on the upside, not just "around 100."

Non-obvious risk: after a large rally (well above 110), P&L is dominated by the extra short 100 call, so you can lose heavily on big upside moves despite thinking you're "long the upside tail."

## 2.1.5: Question 2.5

**Question:** You are making markets in 3-month European options on a stock that pays no dividends. The stock is at 80, interest rates are negligible. The current mid-market quotes (per share) are: 3-month 80 call: 4.0; 3-month 80 put: 3.5. You can trade the stock at 80. 1) Using replication intuition and put–call parity, what synthetic position is priced if you buy the 80 call and sell the 80 put? 2) Compare its cost to trading the analogous stock position. Is there an arbitrage? Describe the trade. 3) Explain how to sanity-check this in an interview by reasoning about payoffs, no formulas.

**Answer:** By put–call parity, long call at strike 80 and short put at 80 replicates a long forward on the stock with delivery price 80, payoff $S_T - 80$. Its cost via options is 4.0 − 3.5 = 0.5 today. Parity says $C - P \approx S - K = 80 - 80 = 0$, so the synthetic forward is overpriced by 0.5. Arbitrage: buy stock at 80, sell the 80 call, buy the 80 put, net cash outlay 79.5. At expiry, whatever $S_T$, you end up with 80 for sure, so you lock in 0.5 riskless profit (ignoring rates). Interview sanity-check: reason that long call + short put at same strike always gives $S_T - K$, i.e., a stock-forward payoff, then compare what you pay for that payoff via options versus directly via the stock.

## 2.1.6: Question 2.6

**Question:** You are interviewing for an equity options role. A junior trader shows you a quote for a 1-year **American** call on a non-dividend-paying stock currently at 50. The strike is 40. Risk-free rates are positive but small (say 2% annualized, continuously compounded is fine conceptually).

They say: "This call is deep in the money; it should be worth at least the stock price minus the strike, so at least 10. But because it's American and you can exercise early, it seems reasonable that the call could be worth more than the stock itself. After all, it's like stock with a free downside floor at 40."

1) Using no-arbitrage and basic payoff arguments (not formulas), explain why an American call on a **non-dividend-paying** stock can *never* be worth more than the stock itself.

2) Given the current stock price is 50, and ignoring minor interest effects, provide a realistic no-arbitrage upper and lower bound for the call's price. Explain each bound in words.

3) How would the argument change (qualitatively) if the stock paid a large known dividend halfway through the year? Why might early exercise then become rational, and how does that affect the upper bound intuition?

**Answer:** If the American call on a non-dividend stock were priced above the stock, say call at $C > 50$, you could short the call, buy the stock for 50, and lock in $C - 50$ risk-free. If exercised, you deliver the stock you already own; if not, you keep the premium. This arbitrage implies call $\leq$ stock, even with early exercise. With $S_0 = 50$, $K = 40$, no dividends, the strict lower bound is intrinsic value, $\max(S_0 - K, 0) = 10$, and the upper bound is $S_0 = 50$, so $10 \leq$ call price $\leq 50$ (in practice, just above 10). With a large known dividend, early exercise can be optimal to capture the dividend, so American > European, but the same arbitrage still enforces call $\leq$ stock.

## 2.1.7: Question 2.7

**Question:** You are given mid quotes for 3-month European calls on a non-dividend-paying stock at 100. Rates are zero. All options have the same maturity.

Strikes and call prices (per share): K = 90: C(90) = 14.5 K = 100: C(100) = 8.0 K = 110: C(110) = 3.0

A junior trader proposes to sell the 90–100 call spread and buy the 100–110 call spread (short 90, long 100, long 100, short 110), claiming the 90 call is overpriced.

1) Using only monotonicity and convexity in strike, check consistency.
2) If inconsistent, construct a static options-only arbitrage from these three calls.
3) Describe the payoff profile and why it is non-negative and strictly positive somewhere.

---

**Intuition:** For European calls on a non-dividend stock with zero rates, as strike $K$ increases, call price $C(K)$ must decrease (monotonicity) and the function $K \mapsto C(K)$ must be convex. Convexity is equivalent to saying that any butterfly (long–short–long at increasing strikes) must have non-negative cost if its payoff is non-negative. If both monotonicity and convexity hold, then with only three strikes there is no static, options-only arbitrage. The junior's "rich skew" view may be a risk-premium story, but not an arbitrage.

---

**Solution:** Monotonicity requires
$$C(90) \geq C(100) \geq C(110).$$

Numerically,

$$14.5 \geq 8.0 \geq 3.0,$$

so monotonicity holds.

Convexity in $K$ for calls means that for three strikes $K_1 < K_2 < K_3$, the discrete second difference satisfies

$$C(K_2) \leq \frac{K_3 - K_2}{K_3 - K_1} C(K_1) + \frac{K_2 - K_1}{K_3 - K_1} C(K_3).$$

Here $K_1 = 90$, $K_2 = 100$, $K_3 = 110$, and $K_2$ is the midpoint, so the right side is just the average of the endpoints:

$$\frac{14.5 + 3.0}{2} = 8.75.$$

Thus convexity demands

$$C(100) \leq 8.75.$$

We have $C(100) = 8.0$, so

$$8.0 \leq 8.75$$

and convexity holds.

Equivalently, consider the 90–100–110 butterfly: long 1 at 90, short 2 at 100, long 1 at 110. Its cost is

$$B = C(90) - 2C(100) + C(110) = 14.5 - 16 + 3 = 1.5 \geq 0.$$

A long butterfly has a non-negative payoff at expiry (zero in the wings, positive in the middle), so paying 1.5 is consistent with no-arbitrage.

Since both monotonicity and convexity hold, any linear combination of these three calls that produces a payoff which is everywhere non-negative must have cost $\geq 0$. Therefore, using only these three options, there is no static options-only arbitrage.

**Common Mistake:** Candidates often misremember convexity, thinking a convex price curve must lie above the chord, which would flip the inequality and wrongly suggest an arbitrage. For call prices as a function of strike, convexity plus decreasingness implies that the discrete butterfly cost $C(90) - 2C(100) + C(110)$ must be non-negative; seeing a positive butterfly price is perfectly consistent with no-arbitrage, not a violation.

## 2.1.8: Question 2.8

**Question:** You are trading 1-year **European** options on a non-dividend-paying stock currently at 120. The continuously compounded risk-free rate is 5% per year... [full question as given].

**Answer:**

Using parity intuition, a long call and short put with strike 120 replicates a long stock financed by borrowing the present value of 120. At $T$, both portfolios pay $S_T - 120$, so today their values must match: $C(120) - P(120) = S_0 - \text{PV}(120)$.

Numerically, $C - P = 14 - 10 = 4$. The bond's PV is $120e^{-0.05} \approx 114.14$, so $S_0 - \text{PV}(120) \approx 120 - 114.14 = 5.86$. The synthetic stock from options plus bond is $4 + 114.14 = 118.14 < 120$, so there is arbitrage: short the stock at 120, buy the call, sell the put, and invest proceeds risk-free, locking in about 2.96 at maturity.

In an interview, draw payoff diagrams: call–put gives $S_T - K$ in all states; stock–bond (stock minus a bond paying $K$)

also gives $S_T - K$. Matching these recovers put–call parity without memorizing the formula.

## 2.1.9: Question 2.9

**Question:** You are looking at 6-month American puts on a non-dividend-paying stock currently at 80. The continuously compounded risk-free rate is 10% per year. Consider the 80-strike put.

1) Using no-arbitrage reasoning and basic payoff logic, derive a realistic lower bound for the 80-strike American put's price today. Explain why it cannot be as high as the present value of 80.

2) Discuss qualitatively when early exercise of an American put does make sense with positive interest rates, and how that affects the relationship between American and European put prices.

3) Suppose the market quoted the 6-month 80-strike American put at 0.10. Argue whether this is consistent with no-arbitrage, and if not, sketch a simple arbitrage strategy using the underlying and borrowing/lending.

**Answer:** The European put lower bound is max(PV($K$) − $S_0$, 0). Here PV(80) = $80e^{-0.05} \approx 76.1$, so PV(80) − 80 $\approx$ −3.9 and the bound is 0. An American put must be worth at least the European, so its lower bound is also 0. It cannot be near PV(80) because 80 is received only if exercised and only when $S_T \le 80$; this payoff is contingent, unlike a guaranteed bond. Early exercise of an American put on a non-dividend stock makes sense when it is very deep in the money and time value is negligible; then getting $K$ early to invest can dominate waiting. This makes American puts at least as valuable as, and sometimes more valuable than, Europeans. A price of 0.10 exceeds the no-arbitrage lower bound of 0 and, with only stock and cash available, does not admit a simple arbitrage; it is just a very low (but not arbitrage-impossible) price.

# Chapter 3: Implied vs. Realized Volatility and Vol Trading Mindset

If you ask a directional trader where they think the market is going, they talk about levels: "S&P to 5300," "EURUSD to 1.10," "Tesla down 15%." If you ask a volatility trader the same question, they answer in a completely different language: "The market's pricing 1-month at 28 vol, I think we'll realize low 20s." They are not betting on where the underlying ends up, but on how violently it gets there and how that violence compares to what is currently priced. This chapter is about adopting that mindset—seeing volatility not as a by-product of price moves, but as an asset that can be quoted, traded, hedged, and mispriced.

The key distinction that structures the entire vol world is implied versus realized volatility. Implied volatility is what the market collectively "believes" about future variability, expressed through option prices. Realized volatility is what actually happens to prices over time. The gap between the two is where traders live. An option with a 1-month implied vol of 25% is really just a statement: "Under current supply, demand, and fear, this is the volatility that makes today's option prices internally consistent." Whether that 25% turns out to be generous, stingy, or wildly wrong will only be known after the month passes and the underlying has traced its jagged path.

Thinking in volatility terms quickly forces you to think in distributions rather than point forecasts. If you sell a 1-week straddle on an equity index, your P&L is not primarily driven by whether the index finishes a bit higher or a bit lower; it's driven by how much it wiggles around in the interim, how that path interacts with your hedging, and how skewed the distribution of moves turns out to be. Two markets might both have "no change" as the most likely outcome, yet in one case the options are cheap because large swings are underpriced, and in the other they are expensive because a whole fan of extreme scenarios has been baked into the vol. Volatility traders care about the shape of that fan.

A surprisingly practical way to internalize this is to think in terms of "breakeven moves." Every option price implies a move in the underlying that roughly justifies paying that premium. For a short-dated at-the-money option, you can often map the implied volatility into an expected one-day or one-week range: "At 30 vol over the next month, the market is saying a ±6% move is 'normal' over that horizon." Interviewers love to press on this intuition: given the current vol and the price of a straddle, what sort of move must occur for the buyer just to break even? If your gut says "There is no way this stock will move that much absent a shock," the option may be rich. If your instinct, informed by recent chaos, says "That's nothing; this thing regularly gaps 10% on headlines," the option might actually be cheap despite looking numerically expensive.

Underneath these judgments lies the vol risk premium, one of the more persistent and curious features of markets. Across equities, FX, rates, and commodities, implied volatility tends to sit above subsequent realized volatility on average. In other words, options are often "overpriced" relative to what happens. This is not a free lunch; it is a reflection of structural forces. Many natural players—insurers, asset managers, corporate treasurers—prefer to buy protection rather than sell it. They will pay up for convexity and crash insurance, just as homeowners pay more for fire insurance than the pure actuarial odds would dictate. The result is that option sellers, who are effectively insuring others against large moves, earn a premium for warehousing that risk, punctuated by painful episodes when the market's worst fears briefly come true and realized volatility explodes far beyond what was implied.

Adopting a volatility mindset also forces you to respect how wrong point forecasts can be. Even if you were granted a magical oracle that told you the exact level of an index in three months, you could still lose money trading options around it. If the path to that final level is bumpier or smoother than the implied volatility suggested, your volatility bet will win or lose regardless of your directional clairvoyance. Legendary blow-ups often trace back to ignoring this: selling options because "nothing will happen" only to discover that "nothing" can be a noisy, P&L-destroying process.

For interview-style problems, this chapter will ask you to wear that vol trader's hat: comparing implied and realized volatility, eyeballing whether options look cheap or rich, and making quick, approximate P&L calculations. You'll be nudged to translate quotes like "20 vol for one month" into concrete breakeven moves, to imagine plausible distributions of outcomes rather than a single guess, and to ask yourself whether you would rather own or be short that distribution at current prices. Over time, you'll start to recognize something that experienced vol traders know well: the market can be roughly right about direction and still be very wrong about the uncertainty around it—and it's in that uncertainty, not the level, that volatility trading opportunities are born.

# 3.1: Interview Questions

## 3.1.1: Question 3.1

**Question:** Given that implied volatility (IV) is a forward-looking metric derived from option prices, and realized volatility (RV) is a backward-looking measure based on historical price movements, how would you assess the potential impact of a significant market event on an option's price, considering the relationship between IV and RV?

**Intuition:** A significant event changes what the market expects, not what has already happened. IV tells you how much movement the market is pricing into options going forward. RV tells you how much the underlying has actually moved. Around big events, IV typically rises before the event (uncertainty is being priced) and then often collapses after the event (uncertainty is resolved), while RV spikes mainly during and immediately after the event. To assess impact on option price, you compare what is being priced (IV) to what is likely to be realized (future RV, informed by past RV and the nature of the event).

**Solution:** Option prices under a model like Black–Scholes are increasing functions of IV. For a call, schematically,

$$C = C(S, K, T, r, \sigma_{\text{IV}}),$$

with

$$\frac{\partial C}{\partial \sigma_{\text{IV}}} > 0.$$

A significant event implies a market-anticipated future volatility $\sigma_{\text{event}}$. Before the event, the IV embedded in the option is $\sigma_{\text{IV, pre}}$. You assess whether

$$\sigma_{\text{IV, pre}} \gtrless \sigma_{\text{expected RV}},$$

where $\sigma_{\text{expected RV}}$ is your forecast of post-event realized volatility, often built from historical RV around similar events plus scenario analysis.

If $\sigma_{\text{IV, pre}} < \sigma_{\text{expected RV}}$, then options are underpricing likely future movement, suggesting that option prices are too low relative to the risk, so buying options (long vega) may be attractive. If $\sigma_{\text{IV, pre}} > \sigma_{\text{expected RV}}$, the market is overpaying for volatility, and option prices are rich, so selling options or volatility strategies may be favored.

After the event, you compare new IV, $\sigma_{\text{IV, post}}$, to the RV realized around the event, $\sigma_{\text{RV, event}}$, to decide if the remaining uncertainty is still overpriced or underpriced.

**Logic:** Start by understanding how much of the event is already priced into IV. Then form a view of how much volatility the event can actually generate, using RV patterns from similar past events and your scenario assumptions. Finally, compare IV to your expected RV to infer whether the option price embeds too much or too little volatility and how its price is likely to react as the event passes and IV normalizes.

**Common Mistake:** Candidates often look only at the absolute level of IV ("IV is high, so options are expensive") without benchmarking it against expected RV. They ignore that high IV can still be cheap if expected realized volatility is even higher, and they forget the typical post-event IV crush that can hurt long options even if the underlying moves in the "right" direction.

## 3.1.2: Question 3.2

**Question:** How does the shape of the implied volatility surface, particularly the steepness of the wings and the skew, inform you about market sentiment and potential mispricings in options?

**Intuition:** The implied volatility surface is the market's "shape" of fear and greed. The skew tells you whether the market is more afraid of crashes or squeezes, and the wings tell you how much the market is willing to pay for extreme scenarios. When that shape deviates from what is economically or statistically reasonable, you may have a mispricing. When it moves sharply, it reveals shifting sentiment about tail risks and directional bias.

**Solution:** Let the implied volatility be $\sigma_{\mathrm{imp}}(K, T)$ as a function of strike $K$ and maturity $T$. The skew is the slope of volatility with respect to strike,

$$\mathrm{Skew}(K, T) = \frac{\partial \sigma_{\mathrm{imp}}(K, T)}{\partial K},$$

and the wing steepness reflects higher-order curvature,

$$\mathrm{Curvature}(K, T) = \frac{\partial^2 \sigma_{\mathrm{imp}}(K, T)}{\partial K^2}.$$

A steep negative skew in equity index options, with higher $\sigma_{\mathrm{imp}}$ for low $K$ put options, signals strong demand for downside protection. This indicates bearish sentiment or elevated crash risk premia: the market is willing to overpay for downside tails. A flatter or even positive skew suggests reduced concern about downside or growing fear of sharp upside moves, often seen in short-squeeze or forced-buying regimes.

Very steep wings, where far OTM calls or puts have much higher $\sigma_{\mathrm{imp}}$ than ATM, often indicate intense demand or supply imbalances in those strikes. If, relative to historical realized volatility and plausible jump or tail models, $\sigma_{\mathrm{imp}}$ on some wing options is excessively high, those options may be overpriced. Conversely, unusually flat or cheap wings can signal underpriced tail risk.

By comparing $\sigma_{\text{imp}}(K, T)$ to your fair model surface (built from expected distributions, jumps, and risk premia), you can identify regions where market prices embed inconsistent or extreme assumptions, highlighting candidate mispricings.

**Common Mistake:** Candidates often read skew only as "directional view" and ignore risk premia and flows. They forget that demand for hedging or regulatory constraints can distort the surface, and they fail to compare the observed surface to a coherent underlying distribution when calling something a mispricing.

### 3.1.3: Question 3.3

**Question:** When comparing two implied volatility surfaces, what can you infer about the market's expectations for the underlying assets based on the shape and steepness of the surfaces?

**Intuition:** An implied volatility surface translates option prices into a "map" of perceived future risk. Where the surface is high, markets expect more uncertainty; where it is low, they expect calmer behavior. The way this surface tilts across strikes and maturities encodes views about fat tails, crash risk, upside potential, and how persistent that risk is over time. Comparing two assets' surfaces is essentially comparing how worried or optimistic the market is about each asset's future distribution.

**Solution:** Let $\sigma_{\text{imp}}(K, T)$ denote implied volatility as a function of strike $K$ and maturity $T$.

If one asset, say A, has a steeper downside skew, meaning $\partial \sigma_{\text{imp}} / \partial K < 0$ is more negative for low $K$ than for asset B, then out-of-the-money puts on A are relatively more expensive. This implies the risk-neutral distribution for A has heavier left tails than for B, i.e., the market assigns higher probability or severity to large downside moves:

$$\text{steep downside skew}$$

$\Rightarrow$ higher crash risk / stronger bearish hedging demand.

A flatter surface in $K$ for asset B, i.e.,

$$\left| \frac{\partial \sigma_{\text{imp}}}{\partial K} \right|_B < \left| \frac{\partial \sigma_{\text{imp}}}{\partial K} \right|_A,$$

suggests a more symmetric or benign view of upside vs downside, indicating more neutral sentiment and less demand for tail protection.

In the maturity direction, if for asset A,

$$\frac{\partial \sigma_{\text{imp}}}{\partial T} > 0$$

and steep, the market expects elevated or persistent volatility in the future. A flatter or downward term structure for B suggests that high volatility, if present, is viewed as more temporary.

Comparing entire surfaces thus reveals relative expectations of tail risk, volatility persistence, and potential mispricings that can be used to construct relative-value or hedging trades.

**Common Mistake:** Candidates often focus only on the level of implied volatility and ignore skew and term structure. They miss that shape and steepness encode tail probabilities, crash fears, and time-dependent risk, not just "more or less volatility."

## 3.1.4: Question 3.4

**Question:** How do you interpret a situation where implied volatility is consistently higher than realized volatility, and what trading strategies might you consider in such a scenario?

**Answer:** When implied volatility (IV) is persistently above realized volatility (RV), the market is consistently overestimating future price variability relative to what actually occurs. This usually means options embed a "volatility risk premium" and tend to be overpriced versus subsequent realized moves. A trader might express a short-volatility view: selling options (e.g., covered calls, cash-secured puts), implementing delta-hedged short straddles or strangles, or using calendar spreads that are net short IV. Position sizing and risk controls are critical, since large jumps or regime shifts can justify high IV, and losses from short-volatility trades can be severe if realized volatility suddenly spikes above the implied level.

## 3.1.5: Question 3.5

**Question:** Explain the concept of the variance risk premium and how it relates to the difference between implied and realized volatility.

**Answer:** The variance risk premium is the compensation investors require for bearing uncertainty about future variance (squared volatility). Formally, it is the difference between the risk-neutral expectation of future variance, inferred from option prices, and the actual realized variance over that period. Implied volatility (IV) reflects the market's risk-neutral expectation and risk compensation, while realized volatility (RV) is the ex post volatility computed from returns. Typically, IV > RV, so the variance risk premium is positive: options are overpriced relative to subsequent realized volatility. This positive premium compensates option sellers for bearing volatility risk and for adverse scenarios where future volatility turns out much higher than anticipated.

## 3.1.6: Question 3.6

**Question:** How does the volatility smile or smirk pattern in the implied volatility surface affect your options trading strategy, particularly in terms of selecting strike prices?

**Answer:** A volatility smile or smirk shows that implied volatility is not flat across strikes: out-of-the-money (OTM) puts often have higher implied volatility than at-the-money (ATM) options, and sometimes OTM calls do too. When IV is elevated at certain strikes, I avoid blindly buying those options since their premiums embed a richer volatility; instead, I may sell them via spreads (e.g., verticals) to harvest that skew. I focus on buying options where IV is relatively low versus the surface (better "volatility value") and selling where IV is rich. Strike selection is therefore guided by where the smile or smirk makes options comparatively overpriced or underpriced in implied volatility terms.

## 3.1.7: Question 3.7

**Question:** In the context of options trading, how do you assess whether an option is underpriced or overpriced by comparing implied volatility to realized volatility?

**Answer:** You compare the option's implied volatility (IV) to the underlying asset's realized (historical) volatility (RV) over a matching horizon. IV is the market's forecast of future volatility embedded in the option price, while RV is what actually occurred in the past. If IV is significantly higher than RV (after adjusting for expected changes and any known events), the option premium likely embeds a volatility "richness" and may be overpriced. If IV is significantly lower than RV, the option may be underpriced. Traders often annualize both, align the lookback window to the option's tenor, and then evaluate IV − RV as a signal for selling (rich) or buying (cheap) volatility.

## 3.1.8: Question 3.8

**Question:** What are the limitations of using implied volatility as a predictor of future realized volatility, and how can traders mitigate these limitations?

**Answer:** Implied volatility (IV) embeds risk premia, supply–demand imbalances, and jump or crash fears, so it often exceeds future realized volatility and is not an unbiased forecast. IV is model- and strike/maturity-dependent (smile, term structure), can move abruptly around events, and may be distorted in illiquid options. It also assumes a specific option-pricing framework that may not match true dynamics. Traders mitigate this by comparing IV to multiple measures of historical volatility, using models with stochastic volatility and jumps, and analyzing the full volatility surface rather than a single IV. They combine IV signals with macro and event risk analysis, diversify option strategies, and enforce strict position sizing and hedging to control forecast error.

## 3.1.9: Question 3.9

**Question:** How does the concept of volatility skew influence your decision-making process when constructing options trading strategies?

**Answer:** Volatility skew shows how implied volatility changes with strike, so it directly shapes strike selection, structure choice, and sizing. If puts have higher implied volatility than calls (equity-style downside skew), I treat out-of-the-money puts as expensive crash protection and consider selling that richness via put spreads, risk reversals, or collars rather than buying naked puts. If the skew is flat or inverted, I'm more willing to buy wings and structure convex payoff profiles (straddles/strangles) because options are relatively cheaper across strikes. Overall, skew guides whether I am a net buyer or seller at specific strikes to exploit mispricing, hedge tail risk efficiently, and improve the strategy's risk-reward.

# Chapter 4: Greeks as Risk Exposures

If you listen carefully on a trading floor, you'll notice that people rarely talk about "Greek letters." They talk about being "long gamma," "short vol," "bleeding theta," or "needing rates to go up." The Greeks are there, of course, but not as symbols from a calculus textbook. They are treated as knobs and levers on a profit-and-loss machine: push the market a little here, and watch the P&L move there. This chapter is about seeing the Greeks the way practitioners actually use them: not as derivatives of a pricing formula, but as risk exposures that explain why your P&L just changed when the world twitched.

Imagine a simple thought experiment: you freeze the entire market for a moment—underlying price, volatility, interest rates, and time—and then nudge just one thing. You move the underlying price by a cent, or you bump volatility by a tiny bit, or you let a single day pass on the calendar. How does your position's value react? The Greeks are nothing more exotic than a structured way of answering that question. Delta tells you how your P&L responds when the underlying wiggles. Gamma tells you how that response itself bends and curves as the wiggle gets larger. Vega is how allergic your position is to volatility shocks. Theta is the slow drip—or, occasionally, the slow reward—of time. Rho is how much you care about the often-forgotten world of interest rates. Together, they form a compact language for telling the story of your P&L when reality moves by just a little.

Curiously, traders often know their Greeks long before they know any option pricing theory. A junior market-maker might be told: "Keep the book flat delta, long a bit of gamma, and don't get too short vega into the weekend." There is no mention of partial derivatives or stochastic calculus, yet this is an extremely precise instruction about risk. Flat delta: you don't want your position to win or lose much if the underlying price drifts a bit. Long gamma: you do want to benefit from big intraday swings, buying low and selling high as you dynamically hedge. Not too short vega: don't build a position that will collapse if volatility jumps unexpectedly on Monday. You can run a multi-million-dollar book on that kind of intuition alone, provided you truly understand the signs and magnitudes of your Greek exposures.

What makes the Greeks particularly powerful is how they interact when the world moves in more than one dimension at once. Real markets don't politely change one variable at a time. The stock rallies, implied volatility drops, rates nudge higher, and another day passes—all before lunch. Your P&L is then a mosaic of small contributions: a bit from delta because the price moved, a bit from vega because vol repriced, some theta from time decay, and an often-underappreciated dollop from gamma because the price move wasn't perfectly linear. Being able to look at your risk report and say, "Given what just happened, my P&L should be about here," and then recognize when reality deviates from that expectation, is the hallmark of a sophisticated risk-taker.

One interesting practical fact: many profitable traders cannot recite the formal definition of gamma, but they are exquisitely sensitive to when they want more of it or less of it. Before major events—earnings releases, central bank meetings, elections—volatility is uncertain and price gaps are likely. A trader who is "long gamma and short theta" may lose money slowly every day the event fails to materialize, but can make it back in a single, wild session when prices lurch and the curvature in their position suddenly pays off. Conversely, a structured product desk selling options to yield-hungry investors might be "short gamma and long theta," collecting steady time decay in quiet markets but exposed to sharp losses if prices break out of their range. Same Greeks, opposite signs, entirely different behavior when the world moves.

Another curious aspect is how differently the very same Greek can feel depending on the product. A long-dated, out-of-the-money option might have a small delta but an outsized vega, so its P&L swings more with changes in implied volatility than with actual moves in the underlying price. Meanwhile, a deep in-the-money short-dated option is essentially a proxy for the stock: huge delta, modest vega, negligible time value. To someone who thinks in formulas, both are "just options." To someone who thinks in exposures, they are radically different creatures, each living and dying by a distinct mix of delta, gamma, vega, theta, and rho.

This chapter will train you to think like that second person. Rather than grinding through the calculus of partial derivatives, we'll repeatedly ask: if price moves a little, vol shifts a bit, and time passes, what should happen to my P&L, and why? You will practice diagnosing P&L from small changes, attributing gains and losses to specific Greeks, and developing an instinct for whether you want to be long or short each exposure in a given scenario. By the end, the Greek letters will recede into the background, and what will remain is a clear, almost tactile sense of how your positions breathe as the market inhales and exhales.

# 4.1: Interview Questions

## 4.1.1: Question 4.1

**Question:** In a portfolio consisting of long call options with varying strike prices, how do delta and gamma interact to influence the portfolio's sensitivity to changes in the underlying asset's price?

**Answer:** In such a portfolio, total delta is the weighted sum of each option's delta and gives the current first-order sensitivity of the portfolio's value to small moves in the underlying price $S$. Formally, portfolio delta is $\Delta_{port} = \sum w_i \Delta_i$. Gamma measures how this portfolio delta changes as $S$ moves: $\Gamma_{port} = \sum w_i \Gamma_i$, and the change in delta for a small change $dS$ is $d\Delta_{port} \approx \Gamma_{port}\, dS$. With long calls of different strikes, gamma tends to be highest near their at-the-money regions, so as $S$ moves, the portfolio's delta can increase or decrease quickly, making the portfolio more convex and more sensitive to further price moves.

## 4.1.2: Question 4.2

**Question:** How does the vega of a portfolio composed of both call and put options with the same strike price and expiration date change when the implied volatility of the underlying asset increases?

**Answer:** For European options in Black–Scholes, vega of a call and vega of a put with the same strike $K$ and maturity $T$ are identical and strictly positive: $\text{Vega} = S\phi(d_1)\sqrt{T}$, where $S$ is the underlying price and $\phi$ is the standard normal density.

In a portfolio holding both the call and the put (same $K, T$), the portfolio vega is the sum of the two positive vegas, so it is positive and does not change sign as implied volatility rises. As implied volatility increases, both option prices rise, and the portfolio's value increases approximately linearly with volatility at a rate equal to its (positive) vega, though the vega itself is largely independent of the volatility level in Black–Scholes.

## 4.1.3: Question 4.3

**Question:** If you hold a short position in a call option and delta hedge by taking a long position in the underlying asset, how does gamma affect the effectiveness of your hedge as the underlying asset's price changes?

**Answer:** In a short call, option gamma is positive, so the position's delta changes nonlinearly with the underlying price. When you delta hedge by going long the underlying, you can only match delta at a point in time. As the underlying price moves by $dS$, delta shifts by gamma $\times$ $dS$, so your hedge quickly becomes imperfect. Higher gamma means delta reacts more strongly to price moves, making the hedge decay in accuracy faster and forcing more frequent rebalancing of the underlying to stay hedged.

## 4.1.4: Question 4.4

**Question:** In a portfolio of options with different expiration dates, how does theta impact the portfolio's overall time decay, and what strategies can be employed to manage this exposure?

**Answer:** Theta measures how much an option's price changes per day from time decay. Portfolio theta is the sum of individual thetas: short-dated options usually have larger (more negative) theta, decaying faster, while longer-dated options decay more slowly and have smaller magnitude theta. As expirations approach, total portfolio theta can accelerate sharply. Traders manage this by structuring offsetting time exposures, most commonly with calendar and diagonal spreads (long longer-dated options, short nearer-dated options) to partially hedge theta. They can also roll short options out in time, diversify expiries, or adjust net theta toward a desired level (e.g., positive for premium sellers, closer to neutral for hedgers).

## 4.1.5: Question 4.5

**Question:** How does rho affect the pricing of options in a rising interest rate environment, and what implications does this have for managing portfolios of interest rate-sensitive options?

**Answer:** Rho is the partial derivative of an option's price with respect to the risk-free rate, $\rho = \partial V / \partial r$. For standard equity options, call $\rho$ is positive and put $\rho$ is negative. As interest rates rise, call prices tend to increase and put prices tend to decrease, all else equal, because the present value of the strike falls and the cost of carry changes. For portfolios, this means net positive $\rho$ benefits from rate hikes, while net negative $\rho$ suffers. Risk management involves measuring portfolio $\rho$, stress-testing for rate shifts, and rebalancing (e.g., via offsetting options, rate futures, or swaps) to keep interest rate exposure within desired limits.

## 4.1.6: Question 4.6

**Question:** In a multi-asset options portfolio, how can aggregating the Greeks across different underlying assets help in assessing the portfolio's overall risk exposure?

**Answer:** Aggregating Greeks by underlying lets you see how the *whole* portfolio responds to key risk factors. By summing delta per asset, you get net sensitivity of portfolio value to each asset's price; summing gamma shows how that sensitivity changes with larger moves; summed vega reveals exposure to volatility shifts; and summed theta shows total time decay. Often, traders also map each asset's

Greeks to common risk factors (e.g., an equity index, a rate curve) and aggregate by factor. This highlights concentrations, offsets long vs short exposures, and enables targeted hedging (e.g., neutralizing net delta or vega) to manage overall portfolio risk coherently.

## 4.1.7: Question 4.7

**Question:** How does the concept of 'position Greeks' differ from 'option Greeks,' and why is this distinction important in portfolio risk management?

**Answer:** Option Greeks are the sensitivities (Delta, Gamma, Vega, Theta, Rho) of a single option's price to risk factors such as underlying price, volatility, time, and rates. Position Greeks are the sum of these Greeks across all options and related instruments in a portfolio, for example total Delta = $\Sigma$ Delta$_i$·quantity$_i$.

**Intuition:** An individual option might be very risky by itself, but in a portfolio its risk can be offset by other positions. Position Greeks reveal the net Delta, Gamma, Vega, etc., guiding how to hedge and ensuring the whole portfolio's exposures, not just single trades, are controlled.

## 4.1.8: Question 4.8

**Question:** In the context of options trading, how does the Black-Scholes model's assumption of constant volatility impact the accuracy of the model's Greeks, and what are the implications for risk management?

**Answer:** Assuming constant volatility, Black-Scholes produces Greeks (delta, gamma, vega, theta, rho) that are internally consistent but often misaligned with real markets where volatility is stochastic, exhibits clustering, jumps, and a smile/skew across strikes and maturities. As a result, delta and gamma hedges can be systematically off, and vega hedges can fail when volatility itself changes unpredictably. This leads to underestimation of tail risk and hedging error, especially during stress. For better risk management, traders calibrate to implied vol surfaces and use models with stochastic or local volatility, scenario analysis, and stress testing rather than relying solely on Black-Scholes Greeks.

## 4.1.9: Question 4.9

**Question:** How can understanding the interaction between delta and gamma help in constructing option strategies that are less sensitive to large price movements in the underlying asset?

**Answer:** Delta measures the sensitivity of an option's price to small changes in the underlying, while gamma measures how fast delta itself changes as the underlying price moves. By combining options so that net delta is near zero (delta-neutral) and gamma is positive, a trader can build a position that is initially insensitive to small moves but responds well to larger moves. Strategies like straddles and strangles use long calls and puts around the current price to create high gamma and low initial delta, making the portfolio less directionally sensitive yet positioned to benefit from large price swings in either direction.

# Chapter 5: Dynamic Hedging, Rehedging Tradeoffs, and Gap Risk

There is a famous quip in options trading: "You're not hedged, you're just hedged at the last tick." Dynamic hedging, in all its mathematical elegance, lives and dies on that uncomfortable truth. This chapter is about operating in the narrow and often dangerous gap between the theory of continuous hedging and the reality of discrete trades, slippage, and markets that occasionally jump instead of glide.

Imagine you begin the day flat delta, long gamma, feeling safe. The model says you can harvest intraday volatility: buy low, sell high, let the gamma do the work. Then the market opens, and prices don't drift—they lurch. An economic surprise hits, the index gaps 2% on the open, liquidity disappears in single names, and your carefully constructed hedge is suddenly misaligned. You are not watching a smooth stochastic process; you are staring at a crime scene. The P&L moves are not the gentle curvature of the Black–Scholes world but jagged cliffs and missing data. This is where dynamic hedging stops being a tidy calculus exercise and becomes a series of judgment calls.

At its core, dynamic hedging is an attempt to manage directional and convexity exposure by continuously rebalancing. The textbook vision is seductively clean: track your delta, trade the underlying, and neutralize directional risk as prices move. In that idealized world of frictionless markets and continuous trading, hedges can be made "perfect" and options can be replicated precisely. Traders learn early, however, that reality charges by the trade, and it charges most when you need it least. Every hedge has a bid–ask spread, an impact cost, and a timing risk. Every decision to rebalance is also a decision to crystallize slippage and invite more trading costs later. The real art is not to hedge, but to decide when not to.

Rehedging frequency is where the theory quietly hands the wheel back to you. Hedge too rarely, and your delta drifts; your book becomes a speculative bet disguised as a risk position. Hedge too often, and transaction costs consume all the gamma you thought would be your friend. In calm markets with tight spreads, leaning toward more frequent rehedging can feel like free money. In volatile, thin markets, the cost of over-hedging can dwarf the theoretical benefits. Curiously, some of the most profitable gamma trading days occur not when you hedge aggressively, but when you intentionally let the book run—accepting some directional pain to avoid paying for every tiny wiggle in the tape.

And then there is gap risk, the elephant in the room that continuous-time models politely ignore. The mathematics assume markets move in infinitely small steps; the market prefers stairs, and sometimes elevators. Overnight earnings, surprise policy moves, flash crashes, and sudden correlation breakdowns create discontinuities that cannot be neutralized by any hedge placed "just before" the move. A delta-neutral book can still be brutally exposed when prices jump beyond the small-change regime your hedge was designed for. Correlations, which quietly underwrite every basket hedge and index overlay, can snap in an instant. The trade that looked like a clean macro hedge at the close can turn into a concentrated idiosyncratic bet by the open.

Some of the most painful episodes in derivatives history are really stories about the limits of dynamic hedging. Portfolio insurance in the 1987 crash was, in spirit, a large-scale dynamic hedging program; when everyone tried to sell into a falling market to "replicate" insurance, they discovered that the underlying liquidity was nowhere near as continuous as the model had assumed. More recently, volatility products designed with beautiful replication arguments unraveled when volatility itself gapped, correlations broke, and the hedges had to be executed into a one-way, crowded market. The models were not wrong in a narrow sense; they were incomplete about the path, the market structure, and the behavior of other hedgers.

This chapter approaches dynamic hedging from the trader's seat, not the blackboard. You will work through a volatile session with a delta-hedged book and see how small timing choices cascade into large P&L swings. You will weigh the tradeoff between being "well-hedged" on paper and quietly bleeding through transaction costs. You will examine scenarios where markets gap, correlations fracture, and liquidity thins just when you need it most, and trace how these frictions push realized outcomes away from the smooth trajectories your model predicted.

By the end, dynamic hedging will look less like a button you press and more like a continuous risk management game played under uncertainty and constraint. The objective is not to eliminate risk—that is impossible—but to understand which risks you are actually running when you rely on dynamic hedges, how those risks behave when markets misbehave, and how to choose rehedging strategies that survive the inevitable gaps between theory and the tape.

# 5.1: Interview Questions

## 5.1.1: Question 5.1

**Question:** You're moderately bullish on a stock over the next month: you think it's likely to drift up 3–5%, but you see a small chance (say 5%) of a sudden 20% gap down on some binary news. The at-the-money (ATM) 1-month call looks fairly priced to you, but the out-of-the-money (OTM) puts 20% below spot look extremely expensive in implied vol terms.

(a) Ignoring funding and dividends, describe a **static option structure** that roughly matches your directional view (benefit from a small grind up) while **selling** what you think is overpriced crash protection.

(b) Now think dynamically: explain, using **payoff replication intuition**, why this structure will behave very differently if you delta-hedge it daily versus leaving it unhedged.

(c) In an interview, how would you argue whether this is genuinely a 'short crash vol' trade or just a 'mildly bullish carry' trade, without writing down any Greeks explicitly?

## Intuition:

You want to be long mild upside, and short what you think is overpriced deep downside insurance. Statistically, you think "small up, rarely big down." Structurally, that is exactly what a risk reversal does: buy upside, sell downside. The key is that the same static payoff can mean two very different risk bets depending on whether you hedge the delta or not. Unhedged, it is mainly a directional bet with an ugly tail. Hedged, it turns into a volatility and jump-risk bet, i.e., short crash volatility.

## Solution:

(a) A natural static structure is a 1-month risk reversal: long an ATM call with strike $K\_ATM \approx S\_0$, short a 20% OTM put with strike $K\_P \approx 0.8S\_0$.

Ignoring cost details, the terminal payoff at maturity $T$ is

$$\Pi\_T = \max(S\_T - K\_ATM, 0) - \max(K\_P - S\_T, 0).$$

If $S\_T$ ends up roughly 3–5% higher, the call gains intrinsic value, and the put is worthless. You benefit from the grind up. If $S\_T$ gaps down by 20% or more, the short put dominates and you lose roughly $K\_P - S\_T$, i.e., you are explicitly short crash protection that you think is overpriced.

(b) Think in terms of replication. A vanilla option can be replicated by a dynamic stock position plus cash. When you delta-hedge frequently, you are constantly adjusting stock to keep the overall delta near zero.

Unhedged, your P&L depends almost entirely on the terminal shape: long upside, short crash downside. You "win" if the path is a gentle drift up and no crash occurs; you "lose big" only if the crash happens.

Delta-hedged, you strip out the directional effect of the 3–5% drift. You lock in something like a pure volatility carry position: you receive premium from the short put, pay premium for the call, and then trade stock to neutralize delta. The residual P&L now comes from realized volatility versus implied. Because the short 20% OTM put has concentrated convexity in the tail, the dynamically hedged position behaves like being short a crash option: you earn small steady carry if the path stays calm, but a sudden 20% gap cannot be hedged continuously, so you incur a large loss when that rare jump happens.

(c) To argue what the trade "really is," stay in payoff language. If you leave it unhedged, the story is: "I make money in the likely scenario of a small up-move; I lose in the unlikely crash. I am expressing a mildly bullish directional view with some negative tail." That sounds like a directional carry trade that incidentally sells crash insurance.

If you delta-hedge, you remove most of the directional benefit of the small drift up. What is left is: "I collect option premium every day as long as the stock does not have a big downside event; if that event happens, I lose a lot at once." In payoff terms, that is equivalent to being short a rare, binary-like crash payoff and long/short some small local convexity around spot. This is better described as a short crash volatility trade, because the main risk you are being paid for is exactly that rare large downside move, not the everyday drift.

**Common Mistake:**
Candidates often describe only the terminal payoff of the risk reversal and call it "bullish with crash risk," forgetting that once you dynamically hedge, you no longer primarily bet on direction. They miss that hedging transforms the position into a volatility and jump-risk exposure, so the same static structure can be either a mild bullish bet (unhedged) or a pure short-crash-vol position (hedged).

## 5.1.2: Question 5.2

**Question:** You are long a 3-month at-the-money (ATM) call and short a 1-month ATM call on the same stock, same strike, same notional (a long calendar spread). You plan to delta-hedge this position daily.

(a) Using replication reasoning, decompose this position into simpler exposures: what are you effectively long and short in terms of **time to maturity** and **volatility path**?

(b) Suppose implied vol is flat across maturities today, but you believe that **over the next month** realized volatility will be low and then pick up strongly in months 2–3. Explain why this calendar spread and your dynamic hedging policy are a reasonably clean expression of that view.

(c) Contrast this with not hedging delta at all: in that case, what hidden directional or gap risks does this structure carry that aren't obvious from the terminal payoff alone?

**Intuition:** The 3-month call minus the 1-month call is like a call that only "lives" from month 1 to month 3: a forward-starting option. Delta hedging strips out direction, so what remains is mostly exposure to how much the underlying wiggles (realized vol) in each time bucket and how implied vol for different maturities evolves.

**Solution:** Statistically, with same strike $K$ and notional, the payoff decomposition is

$$C_{3M}(S_0, K) - C_{1M}(S_0, K)$$

$\approx$ value of a 2-month call starting in 1 month.

In replication terms, you are long a 3-month call (long medium-term gamma/vega) and short a 1-month call (short near-term gamma/vega). With daily delta hedging, you continuously trade stock so that net delta is near zero. The P&L then approximates

$$\text{P\&L} \approx \frac{1}{2} \int_0^{1M} \Gamma_{1M,t} \, d\langle S \rangle_t - \frac{1}{2} \int_0^{3M} \Gamma_{3M,t} \, d\langle S \rangle_t$$

$$+ \text{ theta/vega terms,}$$

so over the first month you are effectively short realized variance (short gamma) via the short 1-month and long a smaller amount of longer-dated variance via the 3-month.

From month 2–3, only the 3-month call remains, so you are outright long gamma/vega there. Net: short near-term vol, long medium-term vol, roughly equivalent to being long a forward-starting 2-month call funded by shorting a 1-month call.

Given your view (low vol in month 1, high in months 2–3), the short 1-month generates positive carry when realized vol is low and you delta-hedge, while the long 3-month benefits if vol and realized variance pick up later. The calendar plus hedging therefore isolates a term-structure view: sell "too-high" near vol, buy "too-cheap" forward vol. Without delta hedging, the structure inherits large spot direction and gap risk. A big move in month 1 can make the short call deep ITM or OTM, generating large losses or gains unrelated to the vol-term view. The expiry of the 1-month call can also leave you with a 2-month call that is far from ATM, so your intended clean long medium-term vol exposure is distorted by the path and level of spot.

**Common Mistake:** Ignoring the path: candidates say "long longer-dated vol, short shorter-dated vol" but forget that without delta hedging, spot trends and gaps in month 1 can dominate P&L and overwhelm the intended volatility-term-structure trade.

## 5.1.3: Question 5.3

**Question:** An institutional client holds a large long stock position and asks you to structure a 6-month zero-cost collar: buy a 10% OTM put and sell a 10% OTM call to finance it.

(a) Using payoff replication intuition (no formulas), explain how this collar can be viewed as transforming the client's stock into a position that is approximately a bond plus a digital exposure to the stock staying within a range.

(b) Suppose the client instead says, "I don't want to cap my upside. Can I keep my stock and just sell you the 10% OTM call, and you give me some other structure that replicates the protection of the put?" Describe, at a high level, what that 'other structure' must look like in payoff terms and what dynamic hedging you'd need to do to keep your own risk similar to the original collar trade.

(c) Interview twist: explain why, even if the two setups have the same terminal payoff for the client, the gap risk and rehedging costs for you as a market maker can be very different.

**Answer:** With the collar, stock plus long put creates a floor: below the put strike the payoff is bond-like, while the short call hands away upside above the call strike. Net, this is like a bond plus a "range-digital" equity exposure that is active only between put and call strikes.

If the client keeps uncapped stock and only sells the call, you must give them a payoff that increases as the stock falls, approximating a long put. You are then effectively short that put and must dynamically delta-hedge: buy stock as it falls, sell as it rises, to mimic the put's curvature.

Despite identical terminal payoff to the client, static options in the collar tightly bound your risk, whereas dynamic replication of the synthetic put is short gamma and exposed to jumps: large gaps break continuous hedging, creating significant gap risk and uncertain rehedging costs.

## 5.1.4: Question 5.4

**Question:** You are choosing between two ways to express a view that the market is underpricing moderate but frequent moves in a stock over the next month, but you are less confident about very large tail events: - Trade A: buy a 1-month at-the-money (ATM) straddle and delta-hedge it frequently. - Trade B: buy a 1-month strangle (same maturity, symmetric OTM strikes) and delta-hedge it in the same way.

(a) Using replication intuition, explain how the gamma and theta profiles of the straddle and the strangle differ as the stock oscillates around the current price, and how that affects your ability to monetize those 'moderate but frequent' moves.

(b) Now think of each structure as a combination of: (i) a central, locally linear exposure, and (ii) digital-like tail pieces. Without writing formulas, describe how you can mentally decompose the strangle into 'short local vol, long tail vol' relative to the straddle when delta-hedged.

(c) Suppose overnight the stock gaps 8% in one direction and then mean-reverts over the next week with choppy 1–2% daily moves. Compare the likely P&L path of the delta-hedged straddle vs strangle in this scenario. Which structure is more aligned with your original view, and why?

**Intuition:** A delta-hedged long option earns or loses money from realized volatility via gamma, and pays for that exposure via theta. An ATM straddle concentrates both gamma and theta right around the current spot, so it is a pure "local vol" bet. A strangle spreads the convexity into the wings: weaker near spot, stronger only when the stock gets close to the OTM strikes. For monetizing frequent moderate moves around today's price, you want the gamma sitting where the stock actually spends time.

**Solution:** Replication intuition says that the delta-hedged option P&L is approximately

$$\text{P\&L} \approx 1/2 \int \Gamma_t S_t^2 \, (dX_t)^2 \, dt \; - \; \int \Theta_t \, dt,$$

with $X_t$ the log-return. Long gamma plus negative theta: you "pay" theta to earn from realized variance.

For a 1-month ATM straddle, both call and put have maximum gamma at spot, so the combined $\Gamma_{\text{straddle}}$ is sharply peaked at the current $S_0$. As $S_t$ oscillates in a 1–2% band around this level, you keep re-delta-hedging: you buy stock when it dips, sell when it rallies. Because gamma is large there, each of these small round-trips generates meaningful P&L. But you also have large $|\Theta|$, so you must harvest enough from these oscillations to beat the time decay.

For a symmetric 1-month strangle, the options start OTM, so their individual gammas are smaller at $S_0$ and peak near the OTM strikes. The combined $\Gamma_{\text{strangle}}$ is flatter and much lower at $S_0$, rising only as $S_t$ approaches the wings. Near today's spot, you have low gamma and relatively modest theta; your delta-hedging on 1–2% moves collects much less realized P&L. You essentially sit in a low-gamma, low-theta position until the stock makes a larger excursion toward a strike.

Mentally, you can take the ATM straddle as the "pure local vol" object. The strangle can be decomposed as: start with that central ATM-like structure and then "cut out" convexity around spot and push it into the tails. Relative to the ATM straddle, the strangle payoff is flatter near $S_0$ and more curved out near the OTM strikes. So, versus the straddle, the strangle is effectively short some central gamma/theta (short local vol) and long extra convexity only once $S_t$ gets into the wings (long tail vol). Under delta hedging, this means you earn less from small oscillations but more if the stock actually runs to or through the OTM levels.

In the 8% overnight gap, the ATM straddle immediately has one deep ITM leg; its value jumps sharply, reflecting long gamma through a large realized move. Your hedge may lag across the gap, but on average a long-gamma, long-vega ATM position benefits from such a move. After the gap, the new ATM is near the new spot, so the straddle again has high gamma there. As the stock mean-reverts with 1–2% choppy moves, you re-hedge frequently and monetize that realized volatility quite efficiently.

For the strangle, the 8% move may bring the spot closer to one OTM strike but not necessarily onto its peak-gamma region. The initial gap gives you some benefit, but per dollar of premium you typically harvest less than the ATM straddle unless the move lands right near a strike. Then, during the 1–2% choppy mean-reversion, the stock likely oscillates between the two OTM strikes, where the strangle's gamma is still relatively low. Your hedging P&L from these moderate moves is therefore muted, while you still bleed some theta.

Your original view is that moderate but frequent moves are underpriced, and you have less conviction about extreme tails. The delta-hedged ATM straddle aligns better with that: it concentrates paid-for optionality exactly where those moderate daily moves occur, making it a focused long local-vol trade. The strangle rebalances risk away from that central zone into the wings, turning it into a relative bet on larger excursions that does not fully exploit the high frequency of moderate moves.

**Common Mistake:** Candidates often say "strangle is just cheaper gamma" and stop there, ignoring where the gamma lives. They miss that for a realized-vol trade with frequent moderate moves, the spatial distribution of gamma and theta matters more than total premium: local convexity around the actual trading range is what drives delta-hedging P&L.

## 5.1.5: Question 5.5

**Question:** You are short a large amount of 1-month at-the-money (ATM) calls on a stock. To manage your risk, you consider buying an OTM call spread (a call butterfly wing): long a call at +5% and short a call at +10%, same maturity.

(a) Ignoring exact Greeks, use payoff and replication intuition to explain how adding this call spread changes your effective exposure to small, medium, and large upside moves, compared to just delta-hedging the short ATM calls.

(b) Now think dynamically: suppose you delta-hedge the entire package (short ATM calls + long 5%/short 10% call spread) daily. Why can this combination be thought of as approximating a short local vol, long medium-range vol, short far-tail vol position? Describe the intuition without equations.

(c) Consider an overnight +7% gap up, followed by a week of sideways trading around the new level. Comparing (i) being only short ATM calls and delta-hedging, versus (ii) being short ATM calls plus the call spread and delta-hedging, explain qualitatively how the P&L and gap risk differ in each case. What common misunderstanding about butterflies does this scenario expose?

**Intuition:** Short ATM calls alone mean you are the insurer of upside: losses grow linearly and then more painfully once gamma bites as the stock rallies. Adding a 5–10% call spread inserts a "patch of long convexity" in the 5–10% region. Below 5% almost nothing changes; between 5–10% your loss profile is softened; beyond 10% you are again largely vulnerable. Dynamically, that spread relocates where your gamma and vega sit: you remain short vol locally, gain long vol in the medium band, and are still exposed to very large jumps.

**Solution:** Let the ATM strike be $K$. Your original position is short calls with payoff at expiry

$$\Pi_{\mathrm{ATM}}(S_T) = -\max(S_T - K, 0).$$

Above $K$ this is a straight line with slope $-1$ and no cap. Add a long call at $1.05K$ and a short call at $1.10K$. The spread payoff is

$$\Pi_{\mathrm{spread}}(S_T) = \max(S_T - 1.05K, 0) - \max(S_T - 1.10K, 0).$$

For small upside moves 0 to $+5\%$, $S_T < 1.05K$, the spread is worthless at expiry, so total payoff is essentially $\Pi_{\mathrm{ATM}}$: you are still just short the ATM call slope.

For medium moves $+5\%$ to $+10\%$, $1.05K < S_T < 1.10K$, so

$$\Pi_{\mathrm{spread}}(S_T) = S_T - 1.05K.$$

This adds a positive slope $+1$ in that band. Net slope becomes about $-1$ from the short ATM plus $+1$ from the long 5% call, so your effective upside exposure between 5–10% is much flatter; the spread absorbs part of the loss.

For large moves above $+10\%$, both wings are in the money, so

$$\Pi_{\mathrm{spread}}(S_T) = (S_T - 1.05K) - (S_T - 1.10K) = 0.05K,$$

a constant. Incremental protection stops growing; your total payoff above $1.10K$ again behaves like a short call (slope roughly $-1$), just shifted by a fixed credit from the spread. Thus small moves: little change. Medium moves: significantly cushioned. Very large moves: you remain exposed, as the spread is capped.

Dynamically, when you delta-hedge, P&L comes from gamma and realized vs implied volatility rather than direction. Near $K$, the 5% call is far OTM, the 10% call even further, so your gamma is dominated by the short ATM calls: you are short local vol. If the stock later trades in the 5–10% band, the long 5% call now has strong gamma, while the 10% call is still relatively mild. In that region, the package is net long gamma, so you can profit from choppy moves: you are long medium-range vol. Once spot moves beyond +10%, both the 5% and 10% calls contribute similar and opposite gamma, so the spread stops giving you net convexity; your profile reverts to being short upside convexity on big tails. That is short far-tail vol.

In the +7% gap scenario, with only short ATM calls, your previous hedge cannot adjust inside the gap. You take a large one-off mark-to-market loss as the calls jump deep in the money. After the gap, if spot sits around +7% and trades sideways, you now have reduced gamma (the call is already ITM), so your ability to earn back losses by re-hedging is limited. Path-wise P&L is dominated by the uncompensated jump.

With the call spread added, the +7% gap lands you inside the spread. The long 5% call jumps into the money and offsets part of the loss on the short ATM calls exactly at the gap, reducing gap risk. Then, during a week of sideways trading near +7%, the long 5% call gives you positive gamma in that area, only partially offset by the still-OTM 10% short. You can scalp that gamma via daily delta-hedging, recovering more P&L.

This exposes a misunderstanding: many think of butterflies or wings purely as static payoff "shapes" that only matter at expiry. In reality, they reallocate gamma and vega across price regions, changing jump risk and how effectively you can monetize post-move volatility.

## 5.1.6: Question 5.6

**Question:** You are trading a non-dividend-paying stock with negligible funding costs. The market shows the following mid quotes for 3-month European options at strike $K = 100$:

- Stock $S = 100$
- 3-month call $C(100) = 6.5$
- 3-month put $P(100) = 7.2$

(a) Using *only* replication and no-arbitrage logic (no formulas), explain why this quote set suggests a violation of put–call parity.

(b) In practice, you are allowed to dynamically hedge your stock position but you cannot short any options. Describe a concrete trading strategy that uses **only stock and the mispriced option(s)** to lock in an almost riskless profit, and explain the residual risk that still remains despite the apparent arbitrage.

(c) Suppose the options were American instead of European. Explain why the **possibility of early exercise** might change your arbitrage logic, and in which direction it would push the *fair* put price relative to the given quote of 7.2.

**Answer:**

**(a) Intuition:** For a non-dividend stock with negligible rates, holding one call plus cash replicates holding one put plus the stock at the same strike and maturity. With $S = K = 100$, call+cash and put+stock must have the same value. That means the call and put should be priced very close. Here the put is 7.2 and the call is 6.5, so the "put+stock" package is richer than the "call+cash" package by about 0.7, indicating the put is too expensive relative to the call and stock, violating parity.

**(b) Strategy and risk:** You cannot short the rich put, so you exploit the cheap call. Buy the call at 6.5 and dynamically short stock against it to keep the position roughly delta-neutral over time. This uses only stock plus the underpriced call. If the put's higher price reflects a higher implied volatility, your call is cheap volatility; as you gamma-trade (repeatedly re-hedge your delta), you can systematically buy low / sell high in the stock, aiming to earn more from gamma than you lose from time decay, giving an almost riskless profit in a smoothly trading market. Residual risks remain: large overnight gaps before you can rebalance, extreme moves that break the small-move replication logic, and the possibility that realized volatility is too low so you just bleed the call's theta.

**(c) American early exercise effect:** For American options, put–call parity becomes an inequality, because the put holder can exercise early when the stock falls far below 100, locking in the strike cash sooner and stopping further downside. This extra flexibility makes an American put strictly more valuable than its European counterpart, while the American call on a non-dividend stock should never be exercised early and so is effectively equal to the European call. Therefore the fair American put price should be **higher** than the European parity level; early exercise pushes the justified put price upward relative to 7.2, softening or potentially eliminating the apparent arbitrage you inferred under pure European logic.

## 5.1.7: Question 5.7

**Question:** You trade options on a stock currently at $S = 50$. In one month, the stock will pay a known cash dividend of 1.0. There are 3-month European options with strike $K = 50$. The continuously compounded risk-free rate is effectively zero.

Market mid quotes: 3-month call, $C(50) = 3.0$ 3-month put, $P(50) = 2.8$

    (a) Using no-arbitrage replication intuition (no formulas), reason whether these prices are roughly consistent with put–call parity after adjusting for the dividend.

    (b) Now suppose the exchange actually lists American options at the same quotes (3.0 and 2.8). A candidate says: "The put is clearly cheap because it can be exercised early, while the call should be cheaper than the European call because you'll lose the dividend." Dissect this.

(c) Describe when an American call on a dividend-paying stock might be exercised early, and link this to no-arbitrage bounds here.

**Intuition:**

For a dividend stock, a long stock plus long put keeps the dividend and gives downside protection. A long call plus cash mimics the payoff at expiry, but you never own the stock before expiry, so you miss the dividend. Relative to the no-dividend case, the call should be cheaper or, equivalently, the put richer by roughly the present value of the dividend.

For American options, early exercise is extra flexibility. That flexibility can never make an option worth less than the corresponding European. The only subtlety is when that flexibility actually has economic value (deep ITM, near ex-div, little time value left).

**Solution:**

For European options with a known dividend $D$ during the life, parity in words is:

"Stock today minus the present value of dividends, plus a put, matches call plus discounted strike."

With rates $\approx 0$, the present value of 1.0 in a month is about 1. The "parity stock" is effectively $S - D \approx 49$. At $K = 50$, this is slightly out-of-the-money for calls and slightly in-the-money for puts, so puts should be at least as expensive as, and plausibly a bit more than, calls. Observed quotes $C = 3.0$, $P = 2.8$ are very close; the 0.2 difference is small versus the 1.0 dividend and well within what you might attribute to volatility skew and bid–ask. So they are roughly consistent with dividend-adjusted parity; not an obvious arbitrage.

For part (b), the claim about the put being "clearly cheap" is overstated. An American put must be worth at least the European put, but equal pricing does not automatically mean mispricing; the early-exercise premium can be tiny for a short-dated, near-ATM equity put. The second part is simply wrong: an American call on the same dividend-paying stock must be worth at least the European call, because you can always choose not to exercise. The candidate is mixing up "call on a dividend-paying stock is cheaper than on a non-dividend stock" (true) with "American vs European on the same stock" (American $\geq$ European).

For part (c), early exercise of an American call is rational just before ex-div when the call is deep in-the-money and its remaining time value is smaller than the dividend you would receive by owning the stock. Formally, just before ex-div, exercise is attractive if

$$C_{\mathrm{mkt}} < (S - K) + D,$$

since exercising gives intrinsic value $S - K$ plus the imminent dividend $D$. In our 3-month, 1.0 dividend case, that condition can only plausibly hold if, one month in, $S \gg 50$ so the call is deep ITM and has little convexity left.

No-arbitrage bounds must reflect that the American call price today must be at least the maximum of intrinsic value now and the discounted value of the best exercise policy around the ex-div date. Symmetrically, the American put must lie between its European value and intrinsic, with the upper/lower bounds constrained so that no combination of early exercise and stock–option trades gives a riskless profit.

---

**Common Mistake:**

Candidates often forget to subtract the dividend from $S$ in parity reasoning and then misinterpret relative call/put richness. A second common error is to think dividends make American calls "worse" than Europeans; in reality, dividends make early exercise potentially optimal, increasing the value of the American relative to the European, not decreasing it.

## 5.1.8: Question 5.8

**Question:** You see the following 2-month European call quotes on a non-dividend-paying stock with $S = 100$, negligible rates:

| Strike K | Call C(K) |
|---|---|
| 90 | 11.3 |
| 100 | 6.0 |
| 110 | 2.5 |

(a) Check whether these prices are consistent with the convexity of call prices in strike. If not, identify the violation.

(b) Construct a static, strike-wise portfolio using only these three calls that produces a non-negative payoff for all terminal stock prices and a positive upfront cash flow. Specify which options you buy/sell and in what quantities.

(c) Now suppose that instead of being able to trade all three strikes, you are only long 100-strike calls (bought at 6.0) and can dynamically hedge with stock. Explain how the convexity violation you just identified would show up as an unusual P&L pattern in your gamma-hedged book compared to what a correctly priced surface would imply.

**Answer:**

**(a)** With equal strike spacing, convexity requires $C(100) \geq [C(90) + C(110)]/2$. Here $[11.3 + 2.5]/2 = 6.9$, but $C(100) = 6.0 < 6.9$, so the call price as a function of strike is locally concave: the 100-strike call is too cheap, violating no-arbitrage convexity.

**(b)** A strike-wise static arbitrage takes the convex combination as a replicating portfolio. Consider long 0.5 of $C(90)$, long 0.5 of $C(110)$, and short 1 of $C(100)$. For any terminal stock price $S_T$, payoff is $0.5(S\_T{-}90)^+ + 0.5(S\_T{-}110)^+ - (S\_T{-}100)^+ = 0$. Initial cost is $0.5 \cdot 11.3 + 0.5 \cdot 2.5 - 6.0 = 6.9 - 6.0 = 0.9 > 0$, so you receive 0.9 up front for zero payoff: a pure arbitrage.

**(c)** If you are just long $C(100)$ at 6.0 and gamma-hedge with stock, a surface consistent with the 90 and 110 quotes would value that call around 6.9. So your book carries underpriced convexity: for a given realized volatility path, the delta-hedged P&L of the 100-strike call will be systematically better (more positive gamma-trading P&L relative to theta decay) than a model calibrated to the wings would predict. The pattern is that your gamma-hedged long call appears "too profitable" versus what a smooth, convex implied-vol surface would allow, revealing the convexity violation indirectly through unusually strong hedged P&L.

## 5.1.9: Question 5.9

**Question:** You are shown a simplified 1-month option quote table on a stock with S = 50, no dividends, negligible rates. All options are European.

Strike | Call C(K) | Put P(K) 45 | 6.0 | 0.8 50 | 3.2 | 2.9 55 | 1.4 | 6.5

(a) Use put–call parity intuition to check whether the 55-strike put at 6.5 is obviously mispriced relative to the 55-strike call and the underlying.

(b) Suppose you can trade all three calls and the stock, but you cannot short puts. Identify any monotonicity or convexity violations in the call strip alone, and outline a static trade (using only calls and stock) that exploits the most egregious one.

(c) In an interview, how would you explain the economic meaning of this mispricing to a non-technical PM who asks, "What kind of scenario is the market overpaying for or underpaying for here?"

**Answer:**

**(a)** Put–call parity with zero rates gives $P(55) \approx C(55) + (55 - S) = 1.4 + 5 = 6.4$. Quoted $P(55) = 6.5$, only 0.1

rich. This is consistent with parity, not an obvious arbitrage.

**(b)** Calls are monotone: $6.0 > 3.2 > 1.4$. Check convexity: $C(50)$ should satisfy $C(50) \geq \frac{C(45)+C(55)}{2} = \frac{6.0+1.4}{2} = 3.7$, but $C(50) = 3.2 < 3.7$. So the 50-call is too cheap. Arbitrage: short a call butterfly using calls only: short $2 \times C(50)$, long $C(45)$ and $C(55)$. Cost: $-6.0 - 1.4 + 2 \cdot 3.2 = -1.0$ (you pay 1), giving a non-negative payoff butterfly. Or equivalently, as given, long $2 \times C(50)$, short $C(45)$, short $C(55)$ gives +1 today with non-positive payoff — same convexity violation.

**(c)** Economically, the market is overpaying for large upside moves (wings at 45 and 55) and underpaying for outcomes where the stock ends near 50. The 50-strike option, which is most valuable if the stock finishes around 50, is too cheap relative to the 45 and 55 calls. So the surface is skewed toward expensive "big move" scenarios and cheap "moderate move/stay-around-here" scenarios. Our trade sells what's overpriced (extreme-move calls) and buys what's underpriced (the at-the-money risk around 50).

# Chapter 6: Structures, Spreads, and Expressing Market Views

In options, the most revealing question is rarely "Is this cheap or rich?" but "What exactly are you trying to say about the market, and where do you want to be wrong?"

Structures and spreads are the language you use to answer that question precisely. They let you turn a vague hunch—"I think it drifts up," "vol feels too high," "the panic is all in the downside"—into a contractually precise bet on direction, volatility, skew, and time.

At first glance, many classic structures seem like mere Lego combinations of calls and puts: verticals, calendars, butterflies, risk reversals, straddles, strangles, collars. But the moment you step into an interview or a trading seat, they stop being cookbook recipes and start behaving more like surgical instruments. The interesting part is not that a bull call spread is "bullish," but that it is bullish only within a very specific price, time, and volatility window, and that someone else—another trader, somewhere—is taking the other side because their window is different from yours.

There is a reason almost every derivatives desk spends an outsized amount of time on what seem like very "simple" trades. A vertical spread, for example, is just two options at different strikes, but it can quietly encode a view on the slope of the implied volatility skew, on whether realized volatility will matter more than carry, and on how close you are willing to live to a payoff cliff. A calendar spread looks like a minor timing tweak, yet it is one of the purest ways to say, "The market has the right idea about where we end up, but the path and timing are mispriced." Butterflies and condors can be read as bets on "nothing happening," but the best traders use them just as often to take a view on the shape of the volatility surface itself.

Some of the most famous real-world trades are, at their core, simple option structures wearing a sophisticated narrative. Equity funds that claim they are "long quality, hedged for tail risk" often turn out to be long stock, short calls, and long puts—a collar with a marketing budget. Commodity producers "locking in" future revenue are typically engaging in variations of verticals and risk reversals. Even central banks, when they implicitly underwrite downside protection for markets, induce flows that get expressed as systematic selling of strangles and buying of downside puts. The building blocks in this chapter quietly sit under trillions of dollars of global risk transfer.

Interviewers love this topic because it forces a candidate to bridge the gap between story and structure. It is one thing to say "I'm mildly bullish but think vol is too high"; it is another to choose between a call spread, a risk reversal, and a covered call, and explain—under pressure—why one structure better matches the view, the constraints, and the client's psychology. Two trades can look similar on day one and yet respond completely differently when the market gaps, time decays, or implied volatilities twist. Understanding that difference is the essence of professional options trading.

Perhaps the most counterintuitive aspect is where the risk actually lives. A long straddle feels "safe" because you are long both wings, but in practice you are betting aggressively on realized volatility and gamma, and you bleed theta every day the world stays boring. A short strangle can feel like "free money" because it wins most of the time—right up until it doesn't, and you discover that you were effectively short disaster insurance. Risk reversals, often sold as tidy directional expressions, are in fact delicate creatures of skew and forward volatility, capable of flipping their P&L drivers as the surface moves beneath you.

Throughout this chapter, the focus will be on using structures to make your view testable and falsifiable. You will be pushed to translate a narrative—"the downside is over-hedged," "earnings will be a nonevent," "the curve is too steep"—into an option structure that makes or loses money for the right reasons. You will compare alternatives that sound similar but load risk into different places: spot vs. vol, level vs. skew, front vs. back end, gap risk vs. grind. And you will see that behind every "simple" spread lies the deeper question a senior interviewer is really asking: Do you understand not just what you want to happen, but how, when, and through which channel you are willing to be wrong?

# 6.1: Interview Questions

## 6.1.1: Question 6.1

**Question:** How would you construct an options strategy to profit from a significant price move in either direction, while minimizing the impact of time decay?

**Answer:** A cleaner way to profit from a big move in either direction while reducing time decay is a long straddle using relatively long-dated options. Buy one at-the-money call and one at-the-money put on the same underlying, with the same expiration and strike $K$ near the current price $S_0$. The payoff at expiration is approximately: profit $\approx |S_T - K| -$ total premium. To reduce theta, choose a longer expiration (higher vega, lower daily theta) and consider taking profits or rolling earlier if implied volatility rises after entry, since much of the edge comes from both movement and possible volatility expansion.

## 6.1.2: Question 6.2

**Question:** Given a moderately bullish outlook on a stock, which options strategy would you employ, and why?

**Answer:** For a moderately bullish view, a bull call spread is appropriate. You buy a call option with a lower strike price $K_1$ and simultaneously sell a call option with a higher strike price $K_2$ (where $K_2 > K_1$), both with the same expiration. This reduces the net premium paid compared with buying a single call, because the premium received from the short call offsets part of the cost of the long call. Your maximum loss is the net premium paid, and your maximum profit is limited to $K_2 - K_1$ minus that net premium, which aligns well with a moderate, not aggressive, bullish expectation.

## 6.1.3: Question 6.3

**Question:** How would you use a risk reversal strategy to express a bearish view on a stock, and what are the potential risks associated with this strategy?

**Answer:** To implement a bearish risk reversal, you sell an out-of-the-money call with strike $K_c$ and buy an out-of-the-money put with strike $K_p$ on the same stock and expiration.

This position benefits if the stock falls below $K_p$, where the long put gains value, and the received call premium can reduce or offset the put cost. However, the short call exposes you to theoretically unlimited loss if the stock rallies well above $K_c$. You also face margin requirements for the short call, potential assignment risk before expiration, and the possibility of loss if the stock trades sideways or falls only slightly, leaving both options near worthless.

## 6.1.4: Question 6.4

**Question:** In a low-volatility environment, how would you implement a butterfly spread, and what is the rationale behind this strategy?

**Answer:** In a low-volatility environment, you implement a long call butterfly by choosing three strikes $K_1 < K_2 < K_3$ (equally spaced) with the same expiry. You buy one call at $K_1$, sell two calls at $K_2$, and buy one call at $K_3$. Net cost is small and defines the maximum loss. The payoff peaks if the underlying finishes at $K_2$, where the short calls are maximally in the money while the wings offset further gains or losses. The rationale is to profit from the expectation that the underlying will stay near $K_2$, i.e., low realized volatility, while limiting risk through a defined maximum loss.

## 6.1.5: Question 6.5

**Question:** How does a calendar spread take advantage of time decay, and in what market conditions is this strategy most effective?

**Answer:** A calendar spread uses opposite positions in the same type of option (call or put) with the same strike but different expirations: you sell the near-term option and buy the longer-term option. Time decay (theta) is faster for the short-dated option, so as time passes, the short option's premium erodes more quickly than the long option's. The net position can gain as the short leg decays, while the long leg still holds time value. This strategy works best in low-volatility, range-bound markets where the underlying price stays near the strike, implied volatility doesn't collapse, and the short option expires with little or no intrinsic value.

## 6.1.6: Question 6.6

**Question:** When would you consider using a long straddle strategy, and what are the key factors to monitor when implementing this approach?

**Answer:** A long straddle is appropriate when you expect a large move in the underlying price but have no directional view, for example before earnings, major economic releases, regulatory decisions, or pivotal company news. You buy a call and a put with the same strike and expiration, profiting if the move exceeds the combined premiums.

Key factors to monitor are implied volatility (IV), time decay, and realized volatility. High IV makes the straddle expensive and raises the breakeven points; rising IV after entry helps, while IV crush hurts. Time to expiration matters because theta accelerates as expiration nears, so you must manage the trade if the anticipated move is delayed.

## 6.1.7: Question 6.7

**Question:** How does an iron condor strategy balance risk and reward, and what are the potential drawbacks of this approach?

**Answer:** An iron condor balances risk and reward by combining a short call spread and a short put spread around the current price. You sell an out-of-the-money call and put, and buy further out-of-the-money call and put for protection. The maximum profit is the net premium received if the underlying price stays between the short strike prices at expiration. The maximum loss is capped and equals the wing width minus the net premium. This creates a high-probability, limited-profit trade with defined, limited risk. Drawbacks include capped upside, sensitivity to large price moves or volatility spikes, assignment risk near expiration, and the need to manage multiple legs and transaction costs.

## 6.1.8: Question 6.8

**Question:** In a market with a steep volatility skew, how would you implement a diagonal spread, and what are the considerations for managing this position?

**Intuition:** A diagonal spread mixes a vertical spread and a calendar spread. You use different strikes and different expiries, same option type. With a steep skew, implied volatility changes sharply across strikes or maturities. You want to be long the "cheap vol" and short the "rich vol," while also letting time decay on the short leg work for you. The trade is really about shaping your exposure to direction, volatility, and theta over time, not just at one expiry.

**Solution:** Consider a bullish call diagonal in an equity index with downside skew. Skew implies lower-strike options have higher implied volatility than higher strikes:

$$\sigma_{\text{impl}}(K_{\text{low}}) > \sigma_{\text{impl}}(K_{\text{high}}).$$

To exploit this with a diagonal, one typical implementation is:

Buy a longer-dated call with strike $K_1$ and expiry $T_2$. Sell a shorter-dated call with higher strike $K_2 > K_1$ and expiry $T_1 < T_2$.

Pricing-wise, the long leg value is

$$C_{\text{long}} = C(S_0, K_1, T_2, \sigma_{T_2}(K_1)),$$

and the short leg value is

$$C_{\text{short}} = C(S_0, K_2, T_1, \sigma_{T_1}(K_2)).$$

Your net debit is

$$\text{Debit} = C_{\text{long}} - C_{\text{short}}.$$

In a steep skew, you choose strikes and expiries so that the option you are long has favorable implied volatility relative to the risk you are short. In equity downside skew, that often means being cautious about selling rich downside vol and preferring structures where your long option has the more convex, less decaying profile.

Risk management focuses on the greeks over time. Theta is dominated by the short leg near $T_1$, so you benefit from time decay as long as spot $S_t$ does not move too far in-the-money on the short option. Vega exposure is mostly from the longer-dated leg, so a rise in longer-dated implied volatility $\sigma_{T_2}$ helps the position, while a drop hurts it. Gamma shifts sharply as $T_1$ approaches; if $S_t$ is near $K_2$, you may need to roll the short call to a later expiry or different strike to control assignment risk and re-balance delta and vega.

**Logic:** Implementation steps are: define directional bias (bullish or bearish), choose the option type (calls for bullish, puts for bearish), select the long expiry and strike to match your longer-term view, then sell a nearer-term option at a strike where you are comfortable potentially having the underlying called away or assigned. You calibrate strikes using the skew: avoid being systematically short the most expensive implied volatility unless you are explicitly betting against it. After entry, monitor how the position's net delta, theta, and vega evolve as the short leg decays, and be ready to roll or close when: the short leg is near expiry, the underlying approaches the short strike, or skew/volatility shifts make your long leg relatively expensive or cheap versus the market.

**Common Mistake:** Many traders look only at the initial payoff diagram and ignore the term-structure and skew dynamics. They underestimate how much the trade's risk profile changes after the short leg expires or moves deep in-the-money, and they fail to manage vega risk on the longer-dated leg if implied volatility normalizes or the skew flattens. They also often place the short strike too close to spot, inviting early assignment and forcing exits at poor prices instead of planned rolls.

## 6.1.9: Question 6.9

**Question:** How does a ratio spread strategy work, and in what scenarios would you consider using this approach?

**Answer:** A ratio spread uses options of the same expiration but different strikes, where you buy fewer contracts and sell more contracts. For example, a call ratio spread might mean buying 1 call at strike $K_1$ and selling 2 calls at a higher strike $K_2$. This often reduces or eliminates net premium paid and can even generate a small credit. You consider a ratio spread when you expect only a moderate move in the underlying and do not anticipate a large breakout. It benefits from time decay on the short options and stable or slightly favorable price movement, but it carries potentially large or unlimited risk if the underlying moves sharply beyond the short strike.

# Chapter 7: Volatility Surface, Skew, and Relative Value Across Strikes and Maturities

In options markets, prices have a habit of telling stories that models never intended. The volatility surface is one of those stories written in real time, in numbers instead of words. On paper, a simple Black–Scholes world would give you a flat line: the same implied volatility at every strike and every maturity. In practice, you see a contoured landscape of smiles, skews, ridges, and valleys that changes from one day to the next. Understanding that landscape—and what it quietly implies about risk, flow, and mispricing—is one of the core crafts of a volatility trader.

The "smile" was first noticed not by theorists, but by traders who saw that out-of-the-money options were stubbornly expensive compared to the model. Equity markets, haunted by crashes, evolved from smiles into steep downside skews: cheap-looking out-of-the-money calls, rich puts, and a persistent premium for insurance against tail events. FX markets, by contrast, often show more symmetric smiles, where both wings can be valuable as participants hedge against regime shifts rather than one-sided crashes. Each asset class carves its own characteristic surface, shaped by who trades it and what they fear.

The vertical slice through this surface—across strikes for a fixed maturity—encodes how the market prices different states of the world: mild moves, big jumps, catastrophic gaps. The horizontal slice—across maturities for a fixed strike—encodes beliefs about how uncertainty evolves with time: central-bank cycles, earnings, elections, regulatory deadlines, or the gradual fading of a crisis. It's no coincidence that the term structure of volatility tends to "kink" around known event dates; the surface is effectively a probability-weighted calendar of market anxiety.

For a relative value trader, the surface is less a picture and more a system of constraints. If you tell me that one particular option is "cheap" or "rich," that statement only makes sense relative to its neighbors on the surface. A single misaligned quote has implications: if a 3-month 25-delta put looks underpriced, then either its nearby strikes must be correspondingly off, or some combination of flies and risk reversals should be misvalued. The logic runs both ways. By examining the shape of flies, you infer the curvature that the market is implying. By looking at risk reversals, you read off the skew: how much the market penalizes downside versus upside. When those elements contradict one another, they flag a possible inconsistency— or a trading opportunity.

One of the curious aspects of this game is how tightly linked everything is by no-arbitrage. You cannot freely assign any set of implied vols to a sequence of strikes and maturities; the surface must obey basic principles like monotonicity of option prices and non-negativity of densities. A too-cheap intermediate maturity sandwiched between two expensive ones suggests that a calendar spread might violate common sense—unless something very special is expected to occur in that time window. A kink or dent in the smile may be telling you about discrete flows or structural supply and demand, but it may also be mathematically incompatible with the rest of the curve if pushed too far.

Traders exploit these relationships through structures that strip out what they don't care about and isolate what they do. A well-crafted butterfly ignores the overall level of volatility and zooms in on curvature across strikes. A risk reversal neutralizes some vega exposure and shines a spotlight on skew. Cross-maturity trades—like long a 1-month option versus short a carefully chosen 3-month—let you express a view on how fast fear will decay or erupt. None of these trades is evaluated in isolation; their value is read against the full geometry of the surface.

What makes this chapter interesting is that it pushes you to think in that geometry. Instead of asking, "Is this implied vol high?" you will learn to ask, "If this vol is right, what must be true about the neighboring strikes and maturities?" When you work through problems on surface shape, flies, risk reversals, and cross-maturity structures, you are effectively reverse-engineering the market's beliefs and searching for logical gaps. By the end, the volatility surface should look less like a mysterious heat map and more like a tightly interwoven fabric—one where any tug at a single point necessarily pulls on many others, and where opportunity lies precisely where those tensions fail to reconcile.

# 7.1: Interview Questions

## 7.1.1: Question 7.1

**Question:** Given an implied volatility surface with a steep curve on the left, indicating that out-of-the-money (OTM) options are very expensive, what does this suggest about market participants' expectations?

**Answer:** A steep left side of the implied volatility surface means low-strike, OTM put options have very high implied volatility and are therefore expensive. This reflects strong demand for downside protection. Market participants are willing to pay a premium for these puts, which implies that they assign a relatively high probability to large negative moves in the underlying asset. In other words, the market is pricing in elevated downside risk and expects that stock prices may fall significantly, or at least wants substantial insurance against such declines.

## 7.1.2: Question 7.2

**Question:** How does a negative volatility skew in equity options reflect market sentiment?

**Answer:** A negative volatility skew means implied volatility is higher for lower strike prices and lower for higher strike prices of the same maturity. This reflects a market that is more worried about sharp downside moves than upside moves. Investors are actively buying downside protection via puts, driving up their prices and thus their implied volatilities. The market is therefore pricing in fatter left tails for the equity return distribution, implying higher perceived crash risk and demand for insurance against significant declines, rather than concern about missing large rallies.

## 7.1.3: Question 7.3

**Question:** As a market maker, how should you adjust your implied volatility surface in response to a trade that affects your inventory?

**Intuition:**

When a trade hits your quotes, your risk changes immediately: your net $\Delta$, $\Gamma$, and especially your vega and skew exposure move. You do not want to re-price only that single strike/maturity in isolation; you want to re-align the whole surface so that: you are less likely to get hit again in the "overloaded" direction, your book is pushed toward a more neutral risk profile, and your prices still look consistent with the rest of the market. In practice this means shifting, tilting, or reshaping the implied volatility surface in a smooth, model-consistent way.

**Solution:**

Let $I(K,T)$ be your implied volatility surface as a function of strike $K$ and maturity $T$. A trade changes your inventory and thus your risk vector

$$R = (\Delta, \Gamma, \text{vega}(T_1, \dots, T_n), \text{ skew, smile, } \dots).$$

Suppose you buy options at strike $K^*$, maturity $T^*$ and become long vega at $(K^*, T^*)$. You now want to sell that risk back to the market, so you make it slightly more attractive for others to sell you less and buy from you more. Concretely, you decrease the bid and increase the ask there in terms of implied vol. On the surface, this is implemented as a local downward adjustment of $I(K^*, T^*)$ for your bid side and upward for your ask side, but in a model you translate this into smooth parameter moves.

If your surface is parameterized, say by a small set of parameters $\theta$ (for example SVI parameters), you choose an update

$$\theta_{\text{new}} = \theta_{\text{old}} + \delta\theta(R)$$

where $\delta\theta(R)$ is computed so that: the new surface reproduces traded prices at $(K^*,T^*)$; risk limits on total vega, skew and wing exposures are respected; and no-arbitrage constraints (monotone call prices, convexity in $K$) remain satisfied. This typically looks like a parallel shift in level for that maturity if your maturity-specific vega is large, plus a skew change if you are unbalanced in OTM puts versus calls.

The core principle is: translate the incremental risk from the trade into a coherent, smooth change of the surface parameters that nudges future order flow in the direction that reduces your inventory imbalance.

**Common Mistake:**

Candidates often move only the traded point's implied vol mechanically, ignoring the need to re-fit the entire surface and to preserve no-arbitrage and smoothness. Another mistake is to adjust prices purely by PnL considerations without explicitly linking the move to the book's risk profile, leading to inconsistent quotes that either invite adverse selection or create static arbitrage.

### 7.1.4: Question 7.4

**Question:** What does the implied volatility surface reveal about the underlying asset's price distribution?

**Answer:** The implied volatility surface encodes the market-implied risk-neutral distribution of future prices. In Black–Scholes with constant volatility, log-returns are normally distributed, so implied volatility is flat across strike and maturity. In reality, the surface is skewed and term-structured: a volatility skew or smile across strikes implies non-normality, specifically skewness (asymmetry of returns) and excess kurtosis (fat tails, higher probability of large moves). The term structure of implied volatility across maturities reflects how tail risk and uncertainty are expected to evolve over time. Thus, the surface indicates that the market expects a return distribution that is asymmetric, heavy-tailed, and state-dependent, rather than Gaussian with constant variance.

### 7.1.5: Question 7.5

**Question:** How does the volatility skew inform us about investor behavior and market expectations?

**Answer:** Volatility skew shows how implied volatility changes with strike price and thus reveals which options investors are most eager to buy or sell. When out-of-the-money puts have higher implied volatility than at-the-money options (a left-skew), it signals strong demand for downside protection, meaning investors fear price drops and expect fatter left tails. A flatter or right-skewed curve can indicate less concern about crashes or more interest in upside calls, as in single-stock options with short-squeeze risk. Overall, the shape and steepness of the skew encode asymmetry in perceived risks, probability of extreme moves, and the market's pricing of crash protection versus upside potential.

## 7.1.6: Question 7.6

**Question:** In a stress scenario where the underlying asset's price decreases by 30%, how should you select appropriate implied volatility changes for options in your portfolio?

**Intuition:** When the underlying drops sharply, markets do not just move the spot; the entire implied volatility surface moves. Typically, volatility rises, downside skew steepens, and short maturities can react more violently than long maturities. You are not guessing a single "new vol number," but constructing a coherent stressed volatility surface consistent with how real markets behave under stress.

**Solution:** Start by defining the stressed spot as
$$S_{\text{stress}} = 0.7\, S_0.$$
You then need a stressed implied volatility surface
$$\sigma_{\text{stress}}(K, T)$$
for strikes $K$ and maturities $T$, not just one volatility.

A practical approach is to work in terms of moneyness, for example log-moneyness
$$m = \ln\left(\frac{K}{S}\right).$$
You want a mapping from the current surface
$$\sigma_0(m, T)$$

to the stressed one. Use historical or scenario-based relationships between spot moves and vol moves. For each tenor $T$, calibrate a model such as

$$\Delta\sigma(m, T) = a(T) + b(T)\, m + c(T)\, \Delta S/S_0,$$

with coefficients derived from past crisis data or from liquid market-implied stress (e.g. index options, variance swaps).

Then define

$$\sigma_{\text{stress}}(K, T) = \sigma_0\left(\ln\frac{K}{S_{\text{stress}}}, T\right) + \Delta\sigma\left(\ln\frac{K}{S_{\text{stress}}}, T\right).$$

Ensure the surface is arbitrage-free (no calendar or butterfly arbitrage) and that skew steepens on the downside: out-of-the-money puts (low $K$ relative to $S_{\text{stress}}$) should see a larger volatility increase than at-the-money options, while far out-of-the-money calls may even see flat or lower vols.

**Logic:** First, move spot to the stressed level. Second, use empirical or model-based rules to increase the overall volatility level and steepen skew, stronger for short maturities. Third, smooth and adjust the surface to remove arbitrage. Finally, reprice all portfolio options using $S_{\text{stress}}$ and $\sigma_{\text{stress}}(K, T)$, ensuring internal consistency across strikes and maturities.

**Common Mistake:** A common error is to add a flat volatility bump to all options or to adjust only at-the-money volatility. This ignores skew, term structure, and the fact that downside options react much more strongly, leading to underestimation of tail risk and mispriced protection in the stress test.

## 7.1.7: Question 7.7

**Question:** How do sticky strike and sticky delta assumptions affect the volatility skew in options pricing?

**Answer:** Under a sticky strike assumption, the implied volatility quoted for a given strike $K$ is held fixed when the underlying price $S$ moves. The volatility surface is viewed as a function $\sigma(K, T)$, so as $S$ changes, options with the same $K$ keep the same IV, and their deltas change. The skew in strike space is stable, but the skew in delta space shifts.

Under a sticky delta assumption, the surface is viewed as $\sigma(\Delta, T)$, so the IV for a given option delta $\Delta$ is fixed. As $S$ moves, the strike $K$ that corresponds to that $\Delta$ is changed to keep IV constant. This makes the skew stable in delta space but moving in strike space, and typically better matches market behavior for short-dated options and risk-management hedging.

## 7.1.8: Question 7.8

**Question:** When pricing a variance swap in a sticky strike world, how should you adjust the fair strike as the underlying asset's price changes?

**Intuition:** In a sticky strike world, the implied volatility surface is assumed fixed in strike space. That means when the spot price $S$ moves, the quoted volatilities as functions of strike $K$ do not change. Since the fair strike of a variance swap is obtained by integrating implied vol over strikes, if the vol surface in strike-space is literally unchanged, the integral is unchanged. So, under the pure sticky-strike assumption, the variance swap fair strike does not move with spot just because $S$ moves. In practice, however, skew and term structure do evolve, so real-world pricing often departs from this idealization.

**Solution:** The fair variance strike $K_{\text{var}}$ (for maturity $T$) under no-arbitrage is given by the log-contract replication formula. Ignoring rates and dividends for clarity, under risk-neutral measure it can be written as

$$K_{\text{var}} = \frac{2}{T} \int_0^\infty \frac{1}{K^2} Q(K)\, dK,$$

where $Q(K)$ is a function of out-of-the-money option prices across strikes, which in turn depend on implied volatilities $\sigma_{\text{imp}}(K)$.

In a sticky strike framework, as spot $S$ changes to $S'$, the mapping $K \mapsto \sigma_{\text{imp}}(K)$ is assumed unchanged:

$$\sigma_{\text{imp,new}}(K) = \sigma_{\text{imp,old}}(K)$$

for all $K$. Then each option price $Q(K)$ stays the same (for unchanged time to maturity and rates), hence

$$K_{\text{var,new}} = K_{\text{var,old}}.$$

Therefore the fair variance swap strike is not mechanically adjusted when $S$ moves if you hold the sticky-strike assumption exact.

In reality, when spot moves, the market volatility surface typically shifts: skew rotates, levels change, and term structure evolves. A more realistic adjustment recomputes $Q(K)$ from the updated surface and re-integrates. Sticky strike is just the limiting case where this recomputation yields the same $K_{\text{var}}$.

**Logic:** Start from the replication formula for variance using a continuum of options. Recognize that fair strike depends only on the cross-section of implied vols as a function of strike. Under sticky strike, this cross-section is invariant to spot. Therefore, the integral and thus the fair variance level stay constant. Any adjustment would come only from deviations from sticky strike, i.e., from actual movements of the surface.

**Common Mistake:** Many candidates confuse sticky strike with sticky delta, and incorrectly shift the vol surface in strike as spot moves. That leads them to change the fair variance strike directly with spot. Under pure sticky strike, you do not re-center the surface in moneyness; you leave it fixed in $K$-space, which means the variance swap fair strike remains unchanged unless the implied vol levels themselves move.

## 7.1.9: Question 7.9

**Question:** How can you implement an arbitrage strategy to profit from discrepancies in the volatility skew?

**Intuition:** Volatility skew means different strikes of options on the same underlying and maturity trade at different implied volatilities. In a "normal" market, the smile or skew has a stable shape. When one part of the skew is "too high" or "too low" relative to the rest (and to historical behavior), you can buy options where implied volatility is cheap and sell options where it is rich, while keeping your position nearly neutral to price moves and overall volatility level. You then profit if the skew shape mean-reverts, even if the underlying price drifts or overall volatility changes.

**Solution:** Consider a single maturity $T$ and an underlying with forward price $F$. Let $K_1 < F < K_2$. Suppose the market quotes implied vols $\sigma_1$ at $K_1$ and $\sigma_2$ at $K_2$, and you believe the "fair" skew would have $\tilde{\sigma}_1, \tilde{\sigma}_2$ with, say, $\sigma_1$ too high and $\sigma_2$ too low.

A simple skew arbitrage is a vertical volatility spread constructed to be delta- and vega-neutral (or close):

You choose quantities $q_1, q_2$ of options at $K_1, K_2$ (calls or puts, same expiry) such that

$$q_1 \cdot \text{Vega}(K_1, \sigma_1) + q_2 \cdot \text{Vega}(K_2, \sigma_2) \approx 0,$$

and possibly

$$q_1 \cdot \Delta(K_1, \sigma_1) + q_2 \cdot \Delta(K_2, \sigma_2) \approx 0.$$

If $K_1$ is overpriced in vol, you short options at $K_1$ and go long options at $K_2$, choosing $q_1, q_2$ from the vega-neutrality equation. The P&L from a small change in implied vols is approximately

$$\text{dP\&L} \approx q_1 \cdot \text{Vega}_1 \, d\sigma_1 + q_2 \cdot \text{Vega}_2 \, d\sigma_2.$$

Given $\text{Vega}_2 = -\frac{q_1}{q_2}\text{Vega}_1$, this becomes

$$\text{dP\&L} \approx q_1 \text{Vega}_1 (d\sigma_1 - d\sigma_2).$$

You profit if the relative move of $\sigma_1$ versus $\sigma_2$ is in the direction of your view: for instance, $\sigma_1$ falls and $\sigma_2$ rises, flattening the skew. This construction can be extended to three or more strikes to isolate pure "curvature" of the skew.

**Logic:** First, identify mispriced segments of the skew by comparing current implied vols across strikes to a historical or model-based reference surface. Second, pick a small set of strikes that capture the mispricing (for example, a low-strike put and an at-the-money call). Third, solve for quantities that neutralize delta and overall vega, leaving the position mainly exposed to relative vol moves between strikes. Fourth, monitor and rebalance as the underlying and vols move, closing when the skew normalizes or your risk limits are hit.

**Common Mistake:** Many candidates confuse skew trades with outright volatility trades, ending up long or short large net vega or delta exposure. Another frequent mistake is ignoring liquidity, bid–ask costs, and model-consistency constraints (e.g., creating an apparent "arbitrage" that disappears once realistic transaction costs and discrete strikes are included).

# Chapter 8: Practical Market Making, Risk Management, and Classic Interview Puzzles

On a real trading desk, the market does not politely line up behind your models. Prices gap on headlines that half the room misreads, clients call just when your risk is most fragile, and your "intuitive" hedge turns out to be short gamma precisely into a volatility shock. This chapter lives in that world. It assumes you have the building blocks of pricing and risk, and then drops you into the messy, fascinating reality of actually making markets, managing a book, and explaining outcomes that don't immediately make sense—even to you.

We begin with the art and discipline of quoting two-sided markets. In theory, a market maker simply posts a bid, posts an ask, earns the spread, and hedges. In practice, every quote is a story condensed into two numbers: your view on fair value, your tolerance for inventory, the urgency of your clients, the behavior of your competitors, and your estimate of how wrong you might be. You will see how a "tight" market can be reckless in one context and conservative in another, why good market makers sometimes intentionally quote "bad" prices to attract or repel certain flows, and how the same spread can feel either razor-thin or luxuriously wide depending on volatility and liquidity. A curious but very real phenomenon you will encounter is that the best traders often worry less about being picked off and more about not being picked off enough—because no interest at all can be a sign your prices are systematically off.

From there, we move into a deliberately quirky options book, the kind you might inherit at 7:32 a.m. from a colleague stuck on a delayed flight. The positions will not be tidy. You may be long upside calls in one expiry, short downside puts in another, and mysteriously flat in vega overall despite feeling very much "long volatility." Then the news hits: a surprise earnings pre-announcement, a regulatory headline, a sudden macro shock. You will have to work through how your P&L changes not just from the underlying move, but from shifting implied vols, skew, and cross-gamma between strikes and maturities. Along the way, you will see why a book can lose money on a day when you were "right" on direction, why traders complain about "winning the wrong way," and how a superficially hedged position can hide nonlinear risks that only show up when the world stops behaving "normally."

A constant theme will be the tension between client flow and risk management. Real desks do not optimize an abstract P&L function; they serve clients, support franchises, and manage relationships. Sometimes the best trade you do all day is one that looks terrible in isolation but earns you the right to see, and selectively internalize, future flow. We will explore situations where you must decide whether to internalize a large client order or pass it on, knowing that either choice could define your day. You will see how a string of "small favours" to clients can quietly transform your risk profile, and why the traders who survive longest tend to obsess over the correlation between the trades they are saying "yes" to.

Interleaved with these scenarios are the puzzles and mental drills that interviewers love and candidates fear: fast approximations, sanity checks, and multi-step risk questions that feel deceptively simple at first glance. There is a reason these puzzles persist at top firms. The point is rarely the exact number; it is whether you can keep a cool head, structure ambiguity, and do robust back-of-the-envelope reasoning when the clock is ticking. You will tackle exercises like inferring whether your book is short gamma just from a few lines of P&L, approximating the impact of a volatility shift without a calculator, or mentally stress-testing a portfolio across correlated moves. A curious historical note: many of the "classic" quant brainteasers were originally internal training games on trading floors, designed by bored but competitive traders trying to outdo each other at lunch.

This chapter will also highlight the common traps that separate strong candidates from merely well-prepared ones. The traps are rarely about obscure formulas. They are about failing to question assumptions, confusing realized and mark-to-market P&L, hedging the wrong risk because a Greek "looks big," or treating client trades as independent when they clearly share a structural theme. You will see how a seductive "perfect hedge" can actually create basis risk that is worse than the original exposure, and why the most dangerous phrase on a trading floor is often "it's probably fine."

By the end, you should feel more comfortable in the grey areas: making imperfect decisions with incomplete information, using mental math to get within a sensible range rather than a false precision, and articulating complex P&L stories in plain language that a risk manager—or an interviewer—can trust. The goal is not to turn you into a market maker overnight, but to help you think like one: aware that every quote is a risk, every hedge is a view, and every puzzle is a rehearsal for the moment when the market turns to you and silently asks, "What's your price?"

# 8.1: Interview Questions

## 8.1.1: Question 8.1

**Question:** You're interviewing for an equity index options market making role.

Spot index is 100. The sales trader calls you: a client wants to buy a 3-month 90–110 call spread (long 90 call, short 110 call, same expiry), and at the same time *sell* you a 3-month 90–110 put spread (short 90 put, long 110 put).

1) Draw or describe the *combined* payoff at expiry of the client's position.

2) Using replication / put-call parity style thinking, simplify this into the payoff of a more familiar structure (or combination of structures). Be explicit about whether it's net long/short underlying, long/short straddle/strangle, etc.

3) From the point of view of the client, what directional and volatility views are they expressing with this package? Answer using signs (bullish/bearish, long vol/short vol) and a short explanation.

You may ignore interest rates and dividends for this question.

**Answer:** The client's payoff at expiry is a constant +20 for all $S_T$: it is 20 when $S_T \leq 90$, 20 for $90 < S_T < 110$, and 20 when $S_T \geq 110$. Using parity, $C(K) - P(K) = S_T - K$. Long

$C(90)$, short $C(110)$, short $P(90)$, long $P(110)$ gives $(S_T - 90) - (S_T - 110) = 20$, independent of $S_T$. So the structure is equivalent to being long a zero-coupon bond paying 20 at expiry. Hence the client is neither bullish nor bearish and is neither long nor short volatility in theory; they are trying to lock in a risk-free 20 via mispricing.

## 8.1.2: Question 8.2

**Question:** You are quoting 1-month options on a stock at 100. A junior trader says: "A symmetric 95–100–105 call butterfly (long 1×95C, short 2×100C, long 1×105C) is just a cheap way to buy gamma near the money."

1) Using replication thinking, decompose this butterfly into simpler, more intuitive pieces (e.g., spreads, straddles, forwards) that make its risk exposures clearer.

2) Based on your decomposition, describe the *directional* and *volatility* exposures of a long 95–100–105 call butterfly, and how they differ from a plain long at-the-money straddle.

3) If the surface is such that out-of-the-money calls are much cheaper in vol terms than the at-the-money call, how does that affect whether the butterfly is relatively attractive or not, compared to a long ATM straddle, for someone who wants to be long gamma but doesn't want to pay much theta?

**Answer:**

**Decomposition:** Write the position as two verticals: long 95C – short 100C plus long 105C – short 100C. So the 95–

100–105 call butterfly is simply a long 95–100 call spread plus a long 100–105 call spread. Equivalently, it is close to "long wide strangle, short tight straddle": long 95C + 105C and short 2×100C.

**Exposures:** Directional: Around 100 the position is near delta-neutral and stays relatively low-delta as spot moves; payoff is peaked at 100 and flat beyond 95 and 105. A long ATM straddle is also locally delta-neutral but quickly becomes strongly directional as spot moves away. Volatility: The butterfly is long gamma but only in a narrow band around 100, and has much lower vega and theta than a long ATM straddle. The straddle is broad long gamma and long vega, benefiting from large moves; the butterfly's profit is localized and capped.

**Cheap wings vs ATM:** If 95C and 105C are cheap in vol while 100C is rich, the butterfly buys cheap wing vol and sells expensive ATM vol. That makes the butterfly a relatively attractive, low-premium, low-theta way to be long localized gamma compared with a pure long ATM straddle, at the cost of a narrower profit zone and limited tail upside.

## 8.1.3: Question 8.3

**Question:** You trade 6-month options on a stock at 100. The market shows strong downside skew: the 80 put is very expensive in implied vol terms compared to the 120 call.

A portfolio manager says: "I am *neutral* on overall 6-month volatility, but I think the *shape* of the skew is wrong. I believe the market is overpaying for crash risk (deep OTM puts) and underpaying for big upside moves. I want a position that: (i) is roughly vega-neutral overall, (ii) is not massively directional at inception, and (iii) benefits if the skew flattens or inverts, regardless of whether overall vol goes up or down."

1) Propose a simple options structure (using vanilla calls/puts on this stock only) that implements this view in a reasonably clean way.

2) Use replication / parity thinking to explain why your structure is approximately vega-neutral but has a strong exposure to skew.

3) Explain qualitatively what happens to your P&L if: (a) the stock drops sharply toward 80, skew steepens further, but overall level of vol stays unchanged; (b) the stock rallies toward 120 and skew flattens because upside calls get bid.

**Intuition:** You want to be short what is rich (downside crash vol) and long what is cheap (upside vol), while keeping total vega and initial directionality small. That is exactly the classic risk-reversal: sell the rich downside put, buy the cheap upside call, with notionals chosen so their vegas roughly cancel. Then your P&L is dominated by how the relative vols of low versus high strikes move, i.e. skew.

**Solution:** Take a 6-month risk-reversal style structure: sell the 80 put and buy the 120 call. Let the notionals be $N_P$ on the 80 put and $N_C$ on the 120 call, chosen so that

$$N_P \, \text{Vega}(80\text{P}) \approx N_C \, \text{Vega}(120\text{C}),$$

which makes total vega close to zero at inception. If needed, you can slightly delta-hedge with stock to keep net delta small, but the core "skew trade" is: short rich downside vol, long cheap upside vol.

From option parity, for any strike $K$ we have

$$C(K) - P(K) = F_0 - Ke^{-rT},$$

which is a synthetic forward with essentially no vega. A long call at a high strike plus a short put at a low strike can be thought of as a combination of forwards at different strikes plus some residual option pieces. Because a forward is vega-free, most of the vega comes from "where on the smile" each option sits. Matching vegas means that if the whole smile shifts up or down (level move in vol), gains on the long-vega 120C are offset by losses on the short-vega 80P, and vice versa. But if skew changes so that downside vol moves differently from upside vol, they no longer offset: you are explicitly short vega in the rich downside region and long vega in the cheap upside region, which is a pure skew exposure.

---

**Logic:** At inception, stock is 100. The 80P is OTM with high implied vol; the 120C is OTM with low implied vol. You construct: short $N_P$ of 80P, long $N_C$ of 120C, with $N_P$ and $N_C$ chosen so that total vega is small and initial delta is manageable, possibly fine-tuned by a small stock hedge. If overall vol level moves up or down uniformly, both $\sigma_{80}$ and $\sigma_{120}$ move similarly. Because $N_P \, \text{Vega}_{80} \approx N_C \, \text{Vega}_{120}$, the structure is approximately vega-flat and you are not taking a big view on the level of vol.

If skew flattens (downside vols fall relative to upside), then the short 80P loses vega value while the long 120C gains vega value. Since you are short vega where vol was too high and long vega where vol was too low, this relative move produces profit even if the average level of vol doesn't change much. Thus your main exposure is to the shape of the smile rather than its level.

**Common Mistake:** Candidates often propose a simple put spread (e.g. long 100P, short 80P) or call spread (long 120C, short 100C). Those structures primarily trade *local* skew between nearby strikes and leave you net long or short vega and quite directional around spot. They do not properly neutralize overall vega nor set up opposing vega at the rich and cheap wings of the smile. The key is to recognize that a risk-reversal, with vegas sized appropriately and delta lightly hedged, is the clean way to isolate skew while staying neutral on the overall level of volatility.

## 8.1.4: Question 8.4

**Question:** You make markets in 3-month options on a non-dividend-paying stock at 100. Interest rates are effectively zero.

A client RFQs you for a 90–110 call spread (long 90C, short 110C). You see in the market that: - 90C is trading at 14 - 110C is trading at 6

1) Using payoff/replication logic (not Black–Scholes), argue whether these prices for the vertical

spread are *plausible* or whether something smells wrong. Be explicit about any arbitrage-like replication you're using.

2) Suppose instead that 90C is at 18 and 110C is at 6. Describe a simple static trade (using only calls, puts, and the underlying) that would lock in a risk-free profit if you could trade at those prices.

3) In an interview, what high-level checks would you mention that a market maker should always apply when seeing quotes like these, before leaning on them?

**Answer:** The 90–110 call spread costs $14 - 6 = 8$, with payoff in $[0, 20]$, so $0 \le 8 \le 20$ and $90C \ge 110C$; these quotes are plausible. With $90C = 18$, $110C = 6$, use parity: $90P = 18 - (100 - 90) = 8$, $110P = 6 - (100 - 110) = 16$. Then the 90–110 put spread costs $16 - 8 = 8$. Call and put spreads with same strikes must have equal price, yet call spread $= 12$, put spread $= 8$. Arbitrage: sell the call spread for 12, buy the put spread for 8, lock in 4 now with zero net expiry payoff. In interview: mention monotonicity, vertical-spread bounds, put-call parity across strikes, and equality of same-strike call/put spreads.

## 8.1.5: Question 8.5

**Question:** You are on an index options desk. A client says: "I think realized volatility over the next month will be much lower than what's implied, but I hate the risk of selling naked straddles. I want to be short vol in a way that: (i) has limited downside, (ii) doesn't require constant delta hedging by me, and (iii) still gives me a decent payout if the index stays in a range."

1) Propose an options structure...
2) Use payoff and replication thinking...
3) What are the main trade-offs versus simply selling an at-the-money straddle and delta-hedging...

**Answer:** A suitable structure is a short iron condor. With index at 100, sell a 95 put and 105 call, and buy an 85 put and 115 call, same expiry, same size. This is a short 95–105 strangle plus long 85 and 115 wings. The core short strangle gives short-vol exposure; the long wings cap the loss so beyond 85 or 115 the payoff is flat, giving finite maximum loss equal to wing width minus net premium. Viewed as two short verticals (short 95–85 put spread and short 105–115 call spread), each has known max loss. Versus an ATM short straddle with delta hedging, you give up theta, vega and potential P&L from active hedging skill, but gain bounded tail risk and no need for continuous hedging.

## 8.1.6: Question 8.6

**Question:** You are making markets in 3-month options on a non-dividend-paying stock. Spot is 100, interest rates are 0. The current screen shows:

3M ATM call ($K = 100$): $C = 7$ 3M ATM put ($K = 100$): $P = 10$

1) Using put–call parity as trading logic, are these consistent with no-arbitrage?

2) If not, construct a static arbitrage using only this call, this put, and the stock, with explicit legs and net cash today.

3) Intuitively, what forward view is implied if both prices are "fair", and why is it absurd?

**Answer:** With $r = 0$ and no dividends, put–call parity as trading logic says the synthetic forward (long call, short put) must equal the actual forward, which here is the spot: long call + short put = long forward at $K = 100$; fair forward = 100, so $C - P$ must equal $S - K = 0$, hence $C = P$. Given $C = 7$, $P = 10$, we have $C - P = -3$, violating no-arbitrage.

Exploit this by buying the synthetic forward and selling the real stock forward: long 1 call (pay 7), short 1 put (receive 10), short 1 share of stock (receive 100). Net cash today is $10 + 100 - 7 = 103$ in. At expiry, this portfolio is guaranteed to pay out exactly 100 (state-independent), so you lock in a risk-free profit of 3.

If you accept both option prices as "fair," you are implicitly accepting an implied forward price $F_{\text{imp}} = K + (C - P) = 100 - 3 = 97$, i.e., the market is saying the fair 3-month delivery price is 97 while spot is 100, with zero rates and no dividends. That would mean you can lock in buying later cheaper than today without any cost, which is impossible in this setup and thus absurd.

## 8.1.7: Question 8.7

**Question:** You trade options on a *non-dividend-paying* stock with spot 100, rates mildly positive but small (say 2%

annualized). You are shown the following prices for 1-year options (all American style unless stated):

- American put, $K = 100$: P_A(100) = 7
- European put, $K = 100$: P_E(100) = 7.2
- American call, $K = 100$: C_A(100) = 9

Assume the European prices are firm and arbitrage-free on the street, and you can trade the underlying and all these options frictionlessly.

1) Explain whether the quoted American put price is consistent with no-arbitrage. If not, describe a specific static or semi-static trade that exploits the inconsistency.

2) Is the American call price obviously wrong relative to the European put and stock? Why or why not? Be precise about any inequalities or bounds you use.

3) Intuitively, for a non-dividend-paying stock, why is early exercise of a *call* almost never optimal, whereas early exercise of a *put* can be rational? How does that intuition connect to the bounds you applied in (1) and (2)?

**Answer:** For any strike and maturity, an American option must satisfy $P_A \geq P_E$. Here $P_A = 7 < 7.2 = P_E$, which violates no-arbitrage. Exploit it by buying the American put at 7 and shorting the European put at 7.2; their payoffs at expiry are identical, so you lock in 0.2 risk-free, while early exercise of the American is under your control.

For calls on non-dividend stock and $r > 0$, early exercise is never optimal, so $C_A = C_E$ in theory and always $C_A \geq C_E$.

Using put–call parity, $C_E = S - Ke^{-rT} + P_E \approx 100 - 98 + 7.2 = 9.2$, so $C_A = 9$ is slightly too low if $r = 2\%$ exactly, but not provably wrong without the exact $r$.

Intuitively, early call exercise destroys time value and forces you to pay $K$ early without gaining dividends, so the extra American flexibility is worthless. For puts, exercising early when deep ITM lets you get $K$ now and invest it, so the early-exercise right has positive value, consistent with $P_A \geq P_E$ and often $P_A > P_E$.

## 8.1.8: Question 8.8

**Question:** You are on a single-stock options desk. Spot $S_0 = 50$. The stock will pay a known cash dividend of 1 in 6 months. You are looking at 1-year European options (maturity $T = 1$ year). The continuously compounded risk-free rate is $r = 4\%$.

Market quotes: 1Y call, $K = 50$: $C = 4.0$ 1Y put, $K = 50$: $P = 3.2$

Discount factors: $e^{-0.04 \cdot 0.5} \approx 0.9802$, $e^{-0.04 \cdot 1} \approx 0.9608$.

Tasks as stated in the prompt.

**Intuition:** With a known dividend, put–call parity says: call minus put equals spot minus the present value of dividends minus the discounted strike. Long call plus short put is a synthetic forward. From the option prices you can back out the forward price the option market is implicitly using, and compare it to the fair forward from spot minus PV(dividend) grown at the risk-free rate. A gap means one forward is "too expensive" versus the other, so you go long the cheap forward and short the rich one.

**Solution:**

Correct put–call parity with one known cash dividend $D$ at $t_d = 0.5$ and maturity $T = 1$ is

$$C - P = S_0 - PV(D) - Ke^{-rT},$$

where

$$PV(D) = De^{-rt_d} = 1 \cdot e^{-0.04 \cdot 0.5} \approx 0.9802.$$

Synthetic forward with delivery price $K$ via long call, short put has present value

$$C - P = e^{-rT}\left(F_{imp} - K\right),$$

so the implied forward is

$$F_{imp} = K + (C - P)e^{rT}.$$

Compute $F_{imp}$:

$$C - P = 4.0 - 3.2 = 0.8, \quad e^{rT} \approx \frac{1}{0.9608} \approx 1.0408,$$

$$F_{imp} \approx 50 + 0.8 \cdot 1.0408 \approx 50 + 0.8326 \approx 50.83.$$

The theoretical fair forward with dividend is

$$F_{theo} = (S_0 - PV(D))e^{rT}.$$

First the prepaid forward:

$$S_0 - PV(D) \approx 50 - 0.9802 = 49.0198,$$

then grow to $T$:

$$F_{theo} \approx 49.0198 \cdot 1.0408 \approx 51.99.$$

So options imply $F_{imp} \approx 50.83$ versus fair $F_{theo} \approx 51.99$. The synthetic forward is too cheap. To arbitrage, you buy the cheap synthetic forward and sell the rich "true" forward via spot and carry.

At $t = 0$, buy the call and sell the put (long synthetic forward at $F_{imp}$). Simultaneously short one share of stock and use part of the proceeds to buy a bond maturing at $t = 0.5$ paying 1 to cover the dividend. The residual cash is invested at the risk-free rate. Economically, this short spot plus carry is being short the fair forward at $F_{\text{theo}}$. You are therefore long a forward at about 50.83 and short a forward at about 51.99, locking in about $51.99 - 50.83 \approx 1.16$ at $T$, risk-free.

**Common Mistake:** People often plug $S_0$ directly into parity and forget to subtract the present value of known dividends. That mis-specifies both the parity and the fair forward, leading them either to miss the arbitrage or to get the trade direction exactly reversed.

## 8.1.9: Question 8.9

**Question:** You are given the following *mid* quotes for 3-month European options on a non-dividend-paying stock with spot S = 100, r ≈ 0. All options have the same maturity.
Calls: - K = 90: C_90 = 11.5 - K = 100: C_100 = 6.5
Puts: - K = 90: P_90 = 1.0 - K = 100: P_100 = 6.0

1) Use put–call parity to check consistency between the 90-strike call and put, and separately between the 100-strike call and put. Are both strikes individually consistent with parity?

2) Even if each strike pair is locally consistent with parity, is the *whole* table globally arbitrage-free? If not, construct a static arbitrage involving at most two options and the stock.

3) In an interview, how would you quickly sanity-check a small options quote table like this for obvious mispricings without doing heavy

calculations? Mention at least two heuristic checks and how they would flag this example.

**Answer:** Put–call parity for a non-dividend stock with $r \approx 0$ is $C_K - P_K = S - K$.

For $K = 90$: $C_{90} - P_{90} = 11.5 - 1.0 = 10.5$ vs $S - K = 100 - 90 = 10$, so parity is off by 0.5.

For $K = 100$: $C_{100} - P_{100} = 6.5 - 6.0 = 0.5$ vs $S - K = 0$, also off by 0.5. Neither strike satisfies exact parity.

Use the $K = 100$ pair: synthetic stock price is $C_{100} - P_{100} + 100 = 0.5 + 100 = 100.5$, above the real $S = 100$. Arbitrage: buy stock at 100, short call 100, long put 100. Initial cost $= 100 - 6.5 + 6.0 = 99.5$. Payoff is always 100, so riskless profit 0.5.

Quick interview checks: mentally compare $C_K - P_K$ to $S - K$; here the 0.5 gap at $K = 100$ stands out. Also check $C_K - P_K + K$ against $S$; seeing 100.5 vs 100 immediately flags a classic parity arbitrage.